The "X" Factor

Personality Traits of Exceptional Science Teachers

The "X" Factor

Personality Traits of Exceptional Science Teachers

by

Clair Berube
Hampton University

Information Age Publishing, Inc.
Charlotte, North Carolina • www.infoagepub.com

Library of Congress Cataloging-in-Publication Data

Berube, Clair T.
  The X factor : personality traits of exceptional science teachers / by Clair Berube.
    p. cm.
  Includes bibliographical references.
  ISBN 978-1-61735-035-1 (paperback) — ISBN 978-1-61735-036-8 (hardcover)
— ISBN 978-1-61735-037-5 (e-book)
  1. Science teachers—Vocational guidance. 2. Science—Study and teaching
—Methodology. 3. Science teachers—Training of. I. Title.
  Q147.B47 2010
  507.1—dc22

                                                            2010012638

Printed in the United States of America

For Teddy

CONTENTS

ACKNOWLEDGMENTS

I would like to thank these individuals for their generous input, who just prove that the bigger you are, the nicer you are. These folks spanned not just the world of science but also education, journalism, feminist studies, and politics. They took time out of their busy schedules to grant me interviews. They are: Carol Gilligan, Howard Gardner, Malcolm Gladwell, Diane Ravitch, Jeffrey Glanz, and one of my favorite scientists, Neil deGrasse Tyson. Thank you to Brian Greene of Columbia University for previous interviews and inspiration. I would like to thank (posthumously) a person that I greatly admired, Frank McCourt, for agreeing to an interview. We never made it to the interview stage, as he succumbed to cancer in July, 2009. But I thought of him often during the writing of this book on teacher greatness. And to all the exceptional teachers out there, whether you do your teaching in a formal classroom, or on a fishing pier with one of your own children, whoever you may be, thanks.

ACKNOWLEDGMENTS

PREFACE

We all know teachers who have had "that certain something" that our other teachers didn't have. They might have known their science, or history, but they also inspired us in ways we still might not comprehend. They got us to understand content that we never thought we could master. They made us feel smart. They taught us so much more than simple academic content. What was it about these gifted individuals that made them stand out in our minds and hearts? Is it something we can easily measure and quantify? Were they taught how to be this way in graduate school? Did they possess inherited talent? Was it learned? Or was it some magical combination of personality and philosophy? We may never know. One thing we do know for sure is that our lives are different and qualitatively better because of them.

Why can some teachers make learning "stick" while others present forgettable lessons? Why do some teachers inspire students to rise to their full potential, while others only inspire contempt? It is intelligence? Charisma? Charm? This book seeks to uncover exactly what that "X" factor is, and how it can be shared by the rest of us mere mortals as we head out every morning to teach America's youth in the currently challenging educational climate. I am myself a science teacher. I taught middle school science in public and private schools for 5 years before becoming a professor of science education. Now I teach people how to teach science (and other general education courses too).

The "X" Factor: Personality Traits of Exceptional Science Teachers
pp. xi–xiv
Copyright © 2010 by Information Age Publishing

I remember back when I was teaching seventh grade life science and we would be studying the anatomy unit. I had the class do all of the usual things one does when teaching life science ... dissect owl pellets, frogs, chicken wings. But something made me think it would be a good idea to take my barely past childhood 12-year-olds to view cadavers at the local medical school as the culminating activity for our anatomy unit. I had prepared them well enough ... they were already familiar with the formaldehyde smell from the frogs and by my description of what they could expect. I told them there was no pressure ... they were free to leave the cadaver room at any time and spend the whole field trip looking at the electron microscopes upstairs. I contacted Dr. Oliver, who at the time was teaching human anatomy to brand-new medical students at Eastern Virginia Medical School. The students he taught had never seen a cadaver before, so he was an expert in easing people into the experience. Dr. Oliver was more than happy to accommodate our brave little troupe.

On the day of our arrival to the medical school, half of the class was sent to the anatomy lab with me, the other half went upstairs to look at specimens through the electron microscopes; then they would switch, while I remained with the new cadaver group. As the students slowly walked into the cavernous, cold antiseptic room with the ominous silver slab tables, in the middle of the room there was one figure, covered from head to toe in a green sheet. Dr. Oliver coaxed the students to gather around the table while he pulled the sheet off of the foot first, then after a while, the leg, until finally as the students became desensitized, the whole cadaver in all of it's glory was uncovered for all to see, to the oohs and aahs of the students and parents. The cadaver's head had been opened and so had the chest and abdomen, which Dr. Oliver reached into on many occasions to retrieve various goodies. Now that the students were eagerly surrounding the table, (leaning *over* it in some cases) they put on their surgical gloves and handed organs back and forth to each other while Dr. Oliver answered the questions of the fascinated students. All fear had vanished, and I was very proud of my little pre-med students. I did this culminating activity for 3 years. I had to get permission from parents of course, but I never had so many parent volunteers for any other field trip all in the years I taught. We had to hire a bus just for the parents!

Once I was wrapping-up a parent-teacher conference with a parent who had accompanied us on the field trip. He was grateful for and had enjoyed the experience and kept expressing to me how he couldn't believe that I had pulled it off. After all, these were just seventh graders, many of whom had never seen a dead body before. As he got up to leave, he said, Ms. Newbold (my name back then), you're nuts! And thank you! (As we both laughed.)

Although this book is aimed at the teaching of science, what I have written here is of use to all teachers teaching in all subject areas. But if we are talking about teacher personalities, it takes a certain personality to successfully teach science and math, which in my opinion need all the help they can get in today's anti-intellectual climate. Science and math inspire fear and dread into the hearts of millions of schoolchildren from coast to coast (and many teachers as well), so as teachers we need to especially "hook" children into these subjects early on, and with the proper attitude, personality and skills, we can do it. The global economy is counting on us.

INTRODUCTION

This book about what makes for a good science teacher probably won't make psychometricians very happy. The science of measurement has not historically been a natural bunkmate of qualitative research. The irony of education as a practice is that the most important aspects of it are the hardest to measure and replicate. The things that matter most can be the hardest to quantify. Recent graduates of medical school are equipped with the latest technologies and treatments, plumbers, carpenters, and contractors know the current trends in home building, even fashion designers know the "formula" for the current fashion trends, and strive to replicate it or to even predict it. But with teaching, it's different. A teacher can graduate from the best graduate school of education at the most expensive university in the country, armed with the latest pedagogical and technological advances. They can know the different learning styles, intelligences, and brain preferences of their students. They can possess the knowledge of how to deliver instruction through cooperative learning, lecture, and constructivist techniques, including teaching in the zone of proximal development, and scaffolding. They can be the champions of PowerPoint and smartboards. They can do all these things and more, but still not ignite the imagination of their students.

But some teachers do. Some teachers can do all of the above, and THEN do something else, but what is it? Some teachers can be the leading researchers in their fields, and leave us flat. What is the recipe for this unique, special teacher? And why is it so hard to explain and describe?

The "X" Factor: Personality Traits of Exceptional Science Teachers
pp. xv–xviii
Copyright © 2010 by Information Age Publishing

We Americans are crazy for measuring success. We have to always be scoring, grading, and ranking everything from colleges to restaurants. We want to be the first, the best, and the most powerful. This is not a bad thing in itself. It propelled us into the space race of the 1950s, and as a result, we were the first to walk on the moon. In keeping with this American spirit, the 1980s saw the rise of a new movement in education, one that would claim excellence reform, and would also require a way to measure this so-called reform. Thus began the standardized testing craze.

Let's look at standardized tests for a moment. These tests are necessary tools for measuring many educational, psychological, and cognitive phenomena, from mathematics and language proficiency (the SAT), to state standardized tests. But how do we measure how well our teachers and schools are performing? Is there a measurement instrument that measures accurately teacher efficacy? Teacher content knowledge? Teacher motivation?

Standardized (high-stakes) tests can undermine the very standards they hope to raise. Just recently in the Norfolk Public School district, a middle school principal came under scrutiny because it was discovered that several of her teachers coached their students for the yearly standardized test, the Virginia Standards of Learning (SOL). Many of the students had the exact same answers during the written portion, word for word. It was also discovered that special education students were omitted from test taking so as not to lower the average score of the school. In an article published in the *Virginian-Pilot* dated December 12, 2009, Amy Jeter wrote this concerning an investigation into the matter:

> The investigation was triggered by a teacher's complaint in June that Principal Cassandra D. Goodwyn pressured teachers to inappropriately direct special education students to an alternative assessment that they were more likely to pass than the Standards of Learning exams. Goodwyn denied the allegation, and state investigators published no conclusion on that specific allegation. Although the investigation was conducted in September and the findings published on Oct. 14, board members first officially heard from school officials about testing irregularities in a Nov. 9 e-mail. That e-mail informed them that *The Virginian-Pilot* was looking into the situation. Most board members didn't receive copies of the state's report until Tuesday, which was two days before the information appeared on PilotOnline.com and the school division held a news conference. Board member Kirk Houston Sr. said Friday that he was "pretty outraged" by the situation. He said he wants to hear from the people involved and make sure they are held accountable. "This is a major, major problem," he said. "I'm anxious to get to the bottom of it." Board member Billy Cook said he was saddened ... and worried about teacher morale. (Jeter, 2009)

This is hardly the problem of Norfolk schools alone. Every single public school system in America has faced similar problems since No Child Left Behind mandated that student success be measured solely by high-stakes standardized tests. There will be more about this in a later chapter.

This book does not qualify as a quantitative measurement of a proven fact. This topic in education is not very sexy, because it relies on digging deeper into the *why* and *how* of teacher greatness, not just the *what*. I cannot prove anything here. I can only seek to explain what makes an inspirational teacher, and in doing so, relay how utterly important this aspect of teaching is in American classrooms. It may actually be the *most important* part of teaching, and alas, the hardest to measure.

PART I

WHAT DO THE EXPERTS SAY ABOUT THIS?
(A REVIEW OF THE LITERATURE)

CHAPTER 1

DISPOSITIONS AND PERSONALITY TRAITS

DISPOSITIONS

Let's begin with dispositions. What are dispositions? We hear about teacher dispositions all of the time, yet we are unsure of exactly what they are. NCATE (National Council for Accreditation of Teacher Education) is the tool that the education profession uses to ensure that colleges and schools of education in universities across America graduate only qualified teachers, by accrediting only those colleges and universities that meet its standards. This is how NCATE (n.d.) defines dispositions:

> Professional attitudes, values, and beliefs demonstrated through both verbal and non-verbal behaviors as educators interact with students, families, colleagues, and communities. These positive behaviors support student learning and development. NCATE expects institutions to assess professional dispositions based on observable behaviors in educational settings. The two professional dispositions that NCATE expects institutions to assess are *fairness* and the belief that all students can learn. Based on their mission and conceptual framework, professional education units can identify, define, and operationalize additional professional dispositions. (para. 17)

The "fuzziness" of teacher dispositions has been noted by scholars of education for some time now. Schussler, Bercaw, and Stooksberry (2003)

The "X" Factor: Personality Traits of Exceptional Science Teachers
pp. 3–12
Copyright © 2010 by Information Age Publishing
All rights of reproduction in any form reserved.

mention the elusive quality of dispositions. "Researchers have not explored effective ways to develop teacher candidate dispositions. If dispositions comprise teacher quality, then development of teacher dispositions is as important as the development of knowledge and skills" (pp. 39-40). They go on to define teachers dispositions as "simple character traits (such as openness to ideas and cheerfulness) or as patterns of behaviors" (p. 40).

We can already see the problem here. Dispositions don't seem easy to objectively define or measure, although academics try to do just that in order to be able to pass this information on to prospective teachers. NCATE seems to describe dispositions as this fuzzy thing that all teachers should have in order to be successful in their profession. But does it really need to be stated that teachers should be fair? That they should believe that students can learn? Isn't that a little like stressing to medical students the importance of believing that their patients are capable of healing? And that if they don't believe that all patients can heal then they ought to find another line of work? It is sort of ridiculous in a way. Of course students can learn. Of course teachers should be fair. So what are we really talking about then when we discuss dispositions? What we are really talking about is the way we each look at the world, philosophy of life, and belief systems. A combination of nature and nurture, and especially personality traits. No wonder we can't easily measure this. It's not an easily measurable thing. How do you quantifiably and objectively measure, assess, and therefore understand, a whole human being?

The reason that the standardized testing movement has proved such a disservice to education, is for this reason alone. Successful education is only partly due to content knowledge, mathematical prowess, and language fluency, which standardized tests *seek* to measure. I say "seek" because in all actuality, they don't even measure them reliably 100% of the time. A student can pass a standardized test, but lack comprehension of the content. (I can already hear the anticonstructivists howling in protest, but more on that later). Much of what makes education "successful" is due to this fuzzy disposition thing, on the part of the student and the teacher. Stressing content over the other part (that I will call the X Factor), only serves to simplify and thereby leads us to misunderstand successful education.

What is successful education? In my opinion it is the transmission of the highest levels of content knowledge, embedded in a problem solving, critical thinking, student-centered, open-ended progressive pedagogy. Constructivism is the philosophy that says that children build knowledge from the platform of prior experiences and modes of thought. It is a progressive educational philosophy that I have described as successful education earlier in this paragraph. There are those in education who dispel constructivism as a lazy pedagogy; one that allows the teacher off the hook where content is concerned. True constructivist teachers know the value of expertise in content, and also how to tie new concepts into exist-ing schema. Now, here I am going to clearly state how unbelievably important content knowledge and expertise is, so that there will be no misunderstanding of what my position is as this book proceeds. This topic will also be fully discussed in chapter 2.

I love science and physics in particular. I taught middle school science for five years, and have been teaching future teachers how to teach sci-ence for the better part of 12 years now, either as a grad student or as a college professor. While most of my normal friends take the latest *New York Times* bestseller to the beach in the summer, I am pouring over the latest treatise on string theory. I believe that science content is so impor-tant, that to prove a point I throw a curveball at my science education stu-dents during the very first class of the semester. I ask them to define gravity. Then I ask for a show of hands as to how many of them know what gravity is. They all raise their hands. Then I ask them to define it. They say that gravity is the force that holds planets in orbit, holds us to the earth, and which controls every object on earth. They seem happy with this definition. Then I say to them, "well, what *is* gravity?" (see Appendix 1 for my complete answer).

"The force of attraction between two or more objects?"

"What exactly is this force?"

"Um … magnetism? The pull of gravity?"

"Incomplete but getting there. Any other guesses?"

I finally deduce that they don't really know what gravity is (and neither for that matter did Isaac Newton). So then I go into my explanation of what gravity really is: a combination of acceleration of the earth (like how you feel in an elevator when you are going up), and the warpage of space-time. Now we dive into quantum mechanics, theoretical physics, Einstein, $E = MC^2$, and even string and M theory. So I am a HUGE stickler for know-ing the latest, most up-to-date *what-is-Brian-Greene-at-Columbia-University-researching-this-week* content knowledge. At this point, the students who have not run out of the door, realize that one cannot be even a fair science teacher without the latest content knowledge. And no offense to English or history fans, but one of the most important aspects of science is its ever-changing nature. So if you are not a serious scientist, no need to apply.

Now that we have that covered, what exactly do these dispositions con-sist of?

PERSONALITY TRAITS

We read previously how Schussler et al. (2003) define dispositions *as* char-acter traits. They listed cheerfulness and openness to ideas as two of these traits. I would like to call these *personality* traits. I will also include psychological traits here, because traits that we possess of a psychological nature define our personality.

Daugherty, Logan, and Turner (2003) conducted a study where they tried to predict successful teaching by identifying psychological traits. Indeed, in their study, they characterize psychological traits as "personality style, creative thinking, and motivation (p. 151). Daugherty et al. reported "documentation accumulated in a variety of other occupational fields (show that) personal qualities have an effect on work performance" (p. 151). So why should this be any different for the teaching profession, arguably the *most* people-centric career there is?

Daugherty et al.'s study is an important one to refer to at this point as we look at predicting successful teachers. They cite a study conducted by Hughes (1987) that used the Myers-Briggs Type Indicator to show a statistical significance between personality as a predictor of teacher burnout. They concluded that extroverted, sensing personality types were more resistive to stress than those styles consistent with feeling and perceptual dominance. Personality also influences patterns of interaction among teachers, their students, and the types of learning environments that emerge from relationships between the two.

The Myers-Briggs Type Indicator (MBTI) has been used successfully for a long time as a tool to assess personality types. The test was first published in 1962 but had been used during World War II by its developers, Katherine Cook Briggs and Isabel Briggs Myers in order to measure personalities of women entering the work force. The test is based on Carl Jung's (1923) theory of personality, which held that people had different personality types. As shown in Table 1.1, there are four scores possible based on certain dichotomies of traits. These are: extroversion versus introversion, sensing versus intuition, thinking versus feeling, and judgment versus perception.

Would all prospective teachers take the test, a person might predict that most of them would be higher on the extroversion than introversion scale. The other scales would be harder to predict. Are teachers who score higher on thinking than feeling better teachers? I myself scored as an "Extrovert, Intuitive, Feeler, Perceiver, or ENFP. These people are described as curious, energetic, adaptable, creative, warm, and caring. Most ENFP's are very empathetic and care more about people than about rules.

What about judgment versus perception? What Daughtery et al. (2003) found was this; 20% of the preservice teachers they tested were scored as extroverted, intuitive, feeling, and perceiving (ENFP) personality type. "The Myers Briggs manual describes individuals with these personality characteristics as enthusiastic, imaginative, intuitive and having a greater range of interests and abilities than any other personality type"(p. 164).

**Table 1.1.   Myers-Briggs Type Indicator
Personality Dichotomies by
Extraversion and Introversion**

Dichotomies	
• Extraversion	• Introversion
• Sensing	• Intuition
• Thinking	• Feeling
• Judging	• Perceiving

Source: Wikipedia (n.d.-a, Four Dichotomies section).

We can see that many teachers have this personality type. But is it *better* than the others in predicting success? According to Daughtery, it is if you want to avoid burnout.

Let's look at the second personality trait mentioned by Daughtery et al. (2003) study, creative thinking or creativity. Most people equate creativity with artists. However, this trait also serves teachers extremely well. (Is teaching not an art?) Good teaching calls for creativity on the part of teachers, or so we hope. According to Daughtery et al., "The art and craft of teaching calls for creativity, imagination, and a philosophical approach that requires students to play with ideas, problems, and concepts" (2003, p. 153). Other research backs this up (Abdallah, 1996; Ducharme & Kluender, 1986; Eisner, 1983).

Daughtery et al. (2003) also believes that creativity *can* be taught in teacher education programs (p. 154). But can we realistically teach such a psychological trait? Daughtery used the Torrance Tests of Creative Thinking (Verbal Form) to measure this trait among 53 preservice teachers in a southeastern university. This test measures creative thinking abilities based on fluency, flexibility and originality. The researchers used a Pearson Product Moment Correlation to measure relationships. The results showed that all three Torrance Tests of Creative Thinking measures (fluency, flexibility and originality) were significantly correlated with classroom performance ratings at the .001 level, which is extremely high in education, which usually only requires a .005 level for significance (p. 60).

Creative people have high levels of self-motivation, or internal motivation. Another term for this is locus of control. Daughtery et al. found this to be the case as well. This is not surprising since creativity calls for self-expression for the sake of expression, and not to please others. And we have flexibility and originality, which these successful teachers possess in varying degrees, and it makes perfect sense. As earlier stated, extroversion and flexibility seem to correlate. Originality goes hand in hand with creativity. Both traits make for happier, if not better, teachers.

Brown (2004) also sought to discover personality preferences that effect teaching. He called these meta programs, and stated that they are "personality preferences that influence, at an *unconscious* level, an individual's language and behavior" [*sic*] (p. 515). Brown also stated that a mismatched meta program could cause student dissatisfaction with the teacher. As listed in Table 1.2, teachers have meta programs, and so do students, and each should be aware of his or her styles to make for happier learning experiences.

In the book *Here's How to Reach Me: Matching Instruction to Personality Types in Your Classroom*, Pauley, Bradley, and Pauley (2002) describe the "Process Communication Model" (PCM), which has been applied not only to education, but to other fields as well: such as business, sales and parenting. The PCM works by "showing teachers which communication style will work best to connect with each student, how to motivate each student individually, and how to resolve conflicts and behavior problems by understanding each students'needs" (p. xi). As shown in Table 1.3, Pauley et al. describe "six different personality types from the perspective of both students and teachers-how they feel, how they think, and how they act" (p. xi), along with their corresponding character strengths and perceptions.

Pauley et al. (2002) states that there are many special education and elementary school teachers in the reactors group, because of their great warmth and compassion. On the other hand, many middle school and high school teachers are workaholics, and use their abilities to think through problems to help their students. There are also many persisters who become middle school and high school teachers. These persisters have a mission of helping others to succeed. Dreamers don't usually become teachers, and I believe that this is a shame. In fact, later in this book, I will proceed to show how people with great imaginations make the best teachers. Rebels are also not represented by high numbers in the teaching profession, probably because of their lack of respect for most authority figures. Teaching requires strict rules and adherence to these rules in most schools, yet one of my favorite teacher role models had a huge disdain for rules … more on that later! (He was also highly imaginative … and a favorite teacher of his students). Many artistic and musical folks don't do well with rules. I believe however, that there should be more Rebels in the teaching ranks. Progressive schools would be a nurturing environment for this type of teacher, as these schools are less bound by standards-based, bubble tests as proof of achievement. If one is a teacher and also has these traits, you can probably find him or her teaching at a college or university.

Finally, promoters are the charmers of the bunch. They are resourceful and adaptable. They love excitement and since they are so charming, they would probably hold the attention of students and get their students to do

Table 1.2.   Illustrations of Brown's Meta Program Behaviors

Pattern	Illustrations of behaviors
Visual	People who exhibit a "visual" preference may: • use "visual" language: words such as focus or clarity; • be fast thought processors; and • talk quickly and adopt an upright posture.
Auditory	An "auditory" preference is indicated by: • language that reflects the qualities of sound, such as tone and pitch; • liking to learn by listening; and • sensitivity to characteristics of speech: tone of voice and rhythm.
Kinaesthetic	An individual with a liking for "kinaesthetic" may: • use "kinaesthetic" language: get to grips with or grasp; • like to learn by movement: writing, highlighting text, doodling, or fidgeting; and • tend to talk more slowly, breathe more deeply than for a "visual" preference.
Detail	A "detail" preference may be indicated by: • a tendency to think inductively, "chunking up" from specifics to abstract concepts; • preferring to receive and disseminate information in small chunks; and • a tendency toward perfectionism.
General	People who prefer to use the "general" mode may: • reason deductively from global concept and "chunking down" to specific details; • want less information, like to get an overview or general impression of a topic; and • can become impatient if anyone tries to give them too much detail.
Options	Individuals with an "options" preference: • are more motivated by options/possibilities; • want to find alternative ways to do things; • like to create procedures and systems, but may have great difficulty following those procedures; and • like to break the rules.
Procedures	A person with a "procedures" preference: • may be motivated to follow a step by step approach; • likes to keep to the rules and do things the right way; • is more interested in how to do things rather than why do them; • will, once a procedure has been started, want to finish it; and • may feel lost or stuck without a procedure.

Source: Brown (2004, p. 517).

more of what they want them to do. Sadly though, according to Pauley, almost NONE of them go on to become teachers. Isn't it interesting that I think that the three personality types *least* inclined to go into the teaching profession, are just the ones that I think *should* go into teaching!

Table 1.3.   Pauley's Six Personality Types

Type	Character Strengths	Perception
Reactors	Compassionate, sensitive, warm	Emotions
Workaholics	Responsible, logical, organized	Thoughts
Persisters	Conscientious, dedicated, observant	Opinions
Dreamers	Reflective, imaginative, calm	Inaction
Rebels	Creative, spontaneous, playful	Reactions
Promoters	Resourceful, adaptable, charming	Actions

Source: Pauly et al. (2002, p. 3).

Jeffrey Glanz, one of the preeminent scholars of educational leadership in the country, speaks to personality styles in his book *Finding Your Leadership Style: A Guide for Educators* (2002). Glanz was inspired by the British philosopher William Hare (1993), who identified virtues he felt should be present in any teacher about to enter the profession, and by Gary Null and his book *Who Are You Really? Understanding Your Life's Energy* (1996). Glanz uses both authors in his book to illustrate the qualities we should possess as teachers. He also included instruments in the back of the book so the reader can self-score his or her own "leadership style," based on personality types.

One of the philosophies Glanz and I both share, is the belief that in the best possible scenario, colleges and universities could select their pool of pre-service teachers based on natural, inherent qualities. How unfortunate is it for a college student to complete a degree program, only to find out that they are not cut out for the classroom? This happens enough as it is when students arrive at their senior year and participate in their student-teaching experiences, where they spend a semester teaching in real classrooms under the guidance of the university supervisor (their professor), and the "regular" teacher in whose classroom the student teacher is working. Glanz (2002) wonders in his book, "Are leaders naturally gifted or can they be 'made'?" (p. 3).

As shown in Table 1.4, Glanz's book is based around seven "qualities" that he gleaned from Null's Natural Life Energy theory. According to Glanz, we feel most comfortable when we use and live by whatever quality we possess.

Glanz describes the primary types of each quality. Dynamics are highly charismatic individuals. Adaptives adapt well to varied situations, although they are neither charismatic nor creative. Creatives are imaginative or have artistic ability. Secondary quality types can be described also: Aggressives can be characterized as highly opinionated or even conten-

Table 1.4. Description of Glanz's Seven Qualities

1. Dynamic aggressives: visionaries; the smallest percentage of the population
2. Dynamic assertives: the change agents, reformers, iconoclasts
3. Dynamic supportives: the nurturing helpers
4. Adaptive aggressives: individuals who aggressively pursue a goal
5. Adaptive assertives: excellent organizers
6. Adaptive supportives: trustworthy, loyal, hard workers; most of the people you'll ever meet
7. Creative assertives: visionary and artistic individuals

Source: Glanz (2002, pp. 3, 4).

tious. Assertives are often secure and confident. Supportives usually exhibit an encouraging and affable nature. According to the instrument I scored as a creative assertive (pp. 5, 6). This was informative and helped me to reflect on who I really am and how it relates to how I perform in college classrooms.

So what about charm? Or charisma? One of the tasks of this book is to convince the reader of my absolute certainty that something fuzzy like charm or charisma, can matter almost more than anything in determining who is successful as a teacher and who isn't. This will be the work of chapter 4.

CHAPTER 2

TEACHER SELF-EFFICACY AND CONTENT KNOWLEDGE

Self-efficacy was first described by Alfred Bandura in his 1977 theory of social learning. Bandura stated that people will do things if they produce a favorable result, or in other words, people will be more apt to pursue an activity if they feel competent and skillful at the activity. Bleicher conducted a study in 2004, whereby he measured science teacher self-efficacy and outcome expectancy in preservice elementary school teachers. The instrument he used was the STEBI-B, or the Science Teaching Efficacy Belief Instrument-Preservice. The STEBI-B measures two constructs based on Bandura's notion of self-efficacy; outcome expectation (the notion that people will perform an action if they believe it will have a favorable result), and self-efficacy (they are confident that they can perform that action successfully (Bleicher, 2004).

Research shows that teachers who lack confidence in what they are teaching, are less likely to teach science (Bleicher, 2004; Ramey-Gassert & Shroyer, 1992). Science is a subject unlike any other in that the nature of science is one of forward movement. In other words, science content is constantly changing, and this can be intimidating to a new teacher, who is trying to juggle so many things at once. Tosun (2000) conducted a study to measure the effects of previous science education courses on science self-efficacy in preservice teachers. "The results suggested that prior science course experience and achievement have little impact on the belief

The "X" Factor: Personality Traits of Exceptional Science Teachers
pp. 13–26
Copyright © 2010 by Information Age Publishing
All rights of reproduction in any form reserved.

systems of future teachers of science" (para. 1). To be more precise,

> It was clear that the discipline-integrated methods course played some role in increasing the science teaching self-efficacy of the pre-service teachers, although their outcome expectancy remain unchanged. The precise influence of the methods course cannot be determined since there were other variables that may have influenced the beliefs of the students. (para. 19)

Tosun (2000) also states that,

> The finding that there were no significant differences between the low group students and the high group students on both the self-efficacy and outcome expectancy scales prior to exposure to the methods course was consistent with Bandura's social cognitive theory ... behavior is shaped by an interaction of behavior, cognitive, and other personal factors, and environment events. Science content knowledge may play a role, but it is not the primary factor that determines the success of a teacher ... this should not be taken as to totally dismiss the role of science content knowledge but, instead, to point to the notion that teacher education programs must be sure to address teacher efficacy beliefs. (para. 23)

What this means is that feeling incompetent in a certain science topic is only *part* of why a teacher may have low self-efficacy. *Beliefs* of whether they can master the content seem to be *just as important* a factor in teacher success. Isn't that what we strive to impart to our students ... the notion that they can do something if they believe they can?

Tosun mentions that biology is the one science content area where pre-service teachers are the most comfortable, and biology courses rank highest in science courses taken at the college level (97% of preservice college students have taken a biology course, as opposed to 29% having taken a physical science course at the university level). Tosun argues that "only superficial knowledge in the various sub-disciplines of science could be expected, so any positive experience with science, such as experienced during the methods course, would undoubtedly produce a positive impact on science teaching and self-efficacy" (para. 25). Murphy, Neil, and Beggs (2007) mention a study Wynne Harlen published in 1995 where she asked teachers to rate their confidence in teaching 11 subjects. Science was ranked eighth, with only music and information technology raking lower than science. And when asked to rank topics in science itself, the physical sciences (physics) ranked the lowest; lower than biology.

Tosun finds fault with science methods courses offered at the university level because of the huge amount of content in each of the disciplines of science. Most methods courses deal mostly with pedagogy and theory. Tosun agrees that because of the lack of science content expertise of most pre-service teachers, content should be addressed more during methods courses. But the depth and breadth of science content makes it impossible for methods courses to handle this, along with teaching pedagogy and theory (2000). This is the reason, in my opinion, that elementary school teachers are so unfamiliar with science content, and more apt to be uncomfortable teaching science. If a person loves science, they will probably major in science and go into one of the science fields. If a person loves science and wants to teach, they will probably become a high school science teacher specializing in either biology, chemistry, physics, or another high school science content area. They could also teach middle school science. A middle school science teacher only teaches science all day, but he or she would teach a variety of science topics, from life science, to earth science and astronomy. It is only at the elementary level where people who do not like science or are uncomfortable with it wind up teaching it. And not all elementary school teachers *dislike* science, but in order to be an effective science teacher, the nature of science calls for competence in the field.

Teacher self-efficacy has been studied for every one of the content areas. But why in particular does science seem to give so many people so much trouble?

TEACHER INTELLIGENCE AND SCIENCE CONTENT

Intelligence certainly is related to self-efficacy in many ways. But extremely smart teachers can still feel inadequate teaching subjects and topics that they are not comfortable with. Is there anyone who thinks that teachers don't have to be intelligent masters of their subject matter? Probably not. In fact, Schussler et al. (2008) equate the importance of teacher dispositions with content knowledge and skills. They also not that "intelligence includes more than ability; it involves an inclination to put one's ability to use and the sensitivity to know when a situation calls for specific skills" (p. 40). I would define "competence" as intelligence plus practical application. Schussler also states that prospective teachers become master teachers when "they become aware of their dispositions across three domains, one of which is intellectual (inclination to think and act around issues related to content and pedagogy)" (p. 40). The other two are cultural and moral.

In chapter 1, I briefly mentioned what I encounter as I begin teaching preservice teachers certain science content. My personal story with physics started earlier however. When I became a middle school science teacher, I was assigned to teach seventh-grade science, which is basically life science, with a unit on astronomy. Physics and astronomy are my favorite subjects in science, so I embarked upon an education in physics, quantum physics, astrophysics, and the like. I did not get much of this content during my science methods courses at the university level, having changed my major from biology to education. I didn't fall in love with physics until after I became a teacher. I had however, taken physics and astronomy during college, and loved it. Over the years I poured over books by Albert Einstein, Stephen Hawking, and Brian Greene in order to learn about physics. I was astounded by what I had to learn that I had not been taught. I want to make clear at this point, that had I wished to become a scientist, and not a middle school teacher, I would have taken all of the required and necessary courses for that major, but as a preservice teacher, this content was severely lacking. And I had what I consider excellent science methods professors! To be fair to my favorite science methods professor, she was a great scientist, and would agree with everything I say here.

In 2008, I wrote an article entitled "Atoms, Strings, Apples and Gravity: What the Average American Science Teacher Does not Teach," where I discussed the lack of sufficient content knowledge by most elementary and middle school science teachers. Especially when it comes to physics and topics like the notion of gravity. As mentioned earlier, biology seems to be the area that gives teachers the most comfort, with physics the most discomfort. Do most teachers think that physics is too difficult for them to learn? We remember learning about gravity as children. We were told that is a force of attraction. As I mentioned earlier, we all think we know what gravity is, but can you actually explain *why* it works?

"But what exactly causes gravity? How do bodies pull on each other? The Newtonian theory of gravity is based on a simple model, one in which bodies attract each other with a force proportional to a quantity called their mass and inversely proportional to the square of the distance between them. This model predicts the motions of the sun, moon, and planets to a high degree of accuracy (Hawking 1988). But while it describes certain components of gravity, it does not explain why objects are attracted to each other. Scientists have known what creates the force we know as gravity for more than one hundred years; however, most lay people do not know it. Einstein said space was not empty but interwoven with time, creating a "fabric" he called *space-time*. Events do not occur in space independent of time. The concept of space-time is difficult to visualize because humans are accustomed to two dimensions, such as diagrams of the surface of the earth (longitude and latitude). And yet, to understand the concept of gravity, we must accept that time and space are not separate entities but are intertwined, forming a fabric affected by the planets and bodies in it. This is known as the theory of relativity" (Hawking, 1988).

When Einstein made this discovery, it changed all of history, not just science. He discovered that gravity has two components, acceleration and mass. Einstein said the pressing force we identify as gravity is merely accelerated motion, much like what we feel in an elevator that is going up. We feel heavier heading toward the penthouse and lighter descending to the lobby. Greene (2004) states, "Einstein realized that gravity and accelerated motion are two sides of the same coin" (p. 65). The feeling of acceleration is indistinguishable from gravity. "Since gravity and acceleration are equivalent, if you feel gravity's influence, you must be accelerating" (p. 67). That is, a person is moving even when sitting still on earth as the earth is hurtling through space at 68,000 miles per hour, therefore, one feels the effects of gravity. Although this explains much of the feeling of gravity, there is yet another aspect that explains the apparent attraction between objects. Einstein found that mass bends and warps the space around it. Photos of sunbeams during total solar eclipses in 1919 and 1922 proved that light bent around the earth as it traveled past. Much like a bowling ball resting on a trampoline, the earth and all matter bend the space around them, accounting for the planets' orbits (see Figure 2.1).

The larger the mass, the tighter the orbit of the planet. That is, just as a larger bowling ball will result in a deeper warp in the trampoline than a smaller bowling ball, a larger planet will make a larger, deeper warp in

Source: PBS Online (n.d.-a).

Figure 2.1.   The Effects of Mass on the Fabric of Space-time. This two-dimensional representation of four dimensional space-time seeks to show how the mass of planets and other objects in space, actually bend and warp the space around them, thereby contributing to orbits and gravity.

space-time than a smaller planet, thereby attracting smaller objects (lesser planets) toward itself. When an object becomes trapped near the larger planet, it results in an orbit around the larger planet (Berube, 2008).

This correct concept of gravity is not taught in most science education classes by science education professors, so how can we expect elementary school teachers to correctly teach the concept of gravity? This is just one example of why so many preservice teachers are scared of science, and unnecessarily so. It isn't properly taught to preservice teachers who are planning to teach science, so in turn, when they have their own science classrooms, they don't teach it properly to the children.

Earlier, Tosun spoke of *beliefs* concerning the ability to teach certain scientific concepts. If a person believes that gravity is beyond their ability to comprehend, then in effect it will be. It is in fact, very easy to learn. I have never included mathematics in my teaching of the concepts of quantum physics, or gravity, (which one would definitely need if studying these topics as a pure science student, or at higher levels). I believe that a person can learn the *concepts* of very high-level science topics, without necessarily knowing the technical aspects of it. This notion has enabled physicists like Stephen Hawking of the University of Cambridge, and Brian Greene of Columbia University, to publish popular books on physics that are targeted for the lay audience. These books have sold millions of copies and have opened up the world of physics to people who are not scientists. I have used their books to teach my college level science methods courses and they have been incredibly useful.

In 2000 I wrote an article entitled "A Conceptual Model for Middle School Science Instruction." In this article, I speak about teaching science in a way that can be understood by everyone, whether they intend to go into the hard sciences or not. I mention teaching Einstein's theory or relativity to middle school science students:

> Picture a middle school science classroom. The students memorize the speed of light and then use this information to convert energy into mass by employing the formula $E = MC^2$. The students forget the memorized information, however, before the red ink on the returned test is dry. Suppose instead that seventh graders were taught Einstein's theory of relativity as a concept before the first formula were taught. Suppose also that only after the students understood the theory conceptually would they then be considered ready to learn the formulas necessary for experimentation and replication. And, having first learned general relativity conceptually, they would then be introduced to related concepts, such as the big bang theory, black holes, quantum gravity, the red shift of light, time travel, and Einstein's famous hypothetical twin paradox. (Berube, 2000, p. 312)

I also mention Stephen Hawking and why his books are so successful:

Most people have mathematical phobias, and that includes fear of formulas of any kind. The renowned physicist Stephen Hawking (1988) knew this when he wrote his famous *A Brief History of Time*. He mentions in the book that his publisher told him that for every formula he included in his book, its sales would be reduced exponentially. Consequently, the only formula in that book is $E = MC^2$. What Hawking does brilliantly is teach the most difficult conceptual ideas to laypeople without using any mathematical formulas, thus allowing them to understand the concepts. (p. 312)

Osborne and Simon (1996) reported that teachers who don't have sufficient content knowledge, or comfort with the content, tend to teach from the textbooks. Teachers who have a greater content competency ask questions, foster class discussions, and pose problems that promote learning and understanding.

As mentioned in the introduction, standardized tests are not the best way to assess open-ended, divergent, creative thinking. Our schools are not set up for conceptual learning, unfortunately. American schools are bubble test-driven, and only standardized test outcomes count. What this overlooks is that if students understand the big concepts, they will also undoubtedly be able to pass a bubble test, not the other way around.

Politicians were left to implement No Child Left Behind under the Bush (G.W.) administration, when accountability for education was the mantra. There is absolutely nothing wrong with accountability, and any school system would agree. The problems arose when accountability relied solely on high-stakes tests. Principals were threatened with job transfer or job loss if results were not acceptable, and the principals would in turn pass this pressure on to their teaching staff, which in turn, would sometimes resort to any means to get their students to pass the tests, including coaching, and "teaching to the test," or teaching to the lowest common denominator; in this case, Bloom's lowest level of learning, the knowledge level (rote memory).

I also did a study that proved this point in 2004, published in an article entitled "Are Standards Preventing Good Teaching?" In this study, I was curious to see how many eighth-grade science students who had recently passed the Virginia SOL (Standard of Learning Test) for physical science, really *understood* the content. So one week after they had taken the test, I gave them my version of the SOL test, which was the exact same test they had taken one week earlier, but this time after each multiple-choice question, I required them to explain or defend their answers. I gave this version of the test to every eighth-grade physical science student in the city of Norfolk, Virginia. When I received my results, I looked at the students who has passed the regular State mandated SOL test, and compared the scores from my test from the same group of passing students. The results were alarming. "[Seventy-one] percent of the students who passed the state mandated, multiple-choice test failed my comprehension test. They either could not explain their answers or gave bogus explanations. It seemed they could pass the SOL but did not understand the subject matter" (Berube, 2004, p. 265). I'm sure the school system did not care much about the students' comprehension level, only that they passed the SOL test. I'm also sure this is true in every school district in America, with few exceptions.

It takes an intelligent teacher to properly teach the concept of gravity. But the vast majority of our teachers are very intelligent. There must be yet another contributing problem. Schools and colleges of education across America have an inferiority complex concerning "being intelligent enough" that is well known among professors and students. Whether it is because of the relatively low pay of the profession, even at the university level, or whether it is the old saying "those that can't do, teach," it is a phantom that is hard to overcome. Many new college students with the highest SAT scores believe this notion and go for the money in other professions. The ones that do go into the teaching field, or who switch their majors over to teaching, are often surprised at how difficult and challenging the content and skill set is to master. Schussler et al. (2008) say of one such student,

> Jackie has always liked school, which is why she chose teaching as a profession, despite her father's wishes to follow in his footsteps and become a doctor. Although she knows she is intelligent enough to be a doctor and she would be able to care for others had she chosen this career path, Jackie knows she is right where she is supposed to be (in the education field). (p. 49)

Intelligent enough to be a doctor? What about intelligent enough to be a teacher?

Part of this intellectual ability needed for teaching posited by Schussler et al. is "knowing students and making appropriate instructional decisions" and how to participate in "student motivation" (2008, p. 42), which is also the idea behind Pauley et al.'s Process Communication Model of teacher and student personalities (2002) mentioned in chapter 1 (see Table 1.3). How does Schussler suggest that knowing students is part of teacher intelligence? When a teacher is "inclined to consider the instructional methods to increase student interest"(p. 42), which is what motivation is all about.

Content is of the utmost importance, but there is another piece of the puzzle. Many teachers labor under the assumption that as long as they stick to their subject matter and content area, then they are doing their job (p. 44). This implies a surface knowledge of their students, and a lack of sensitivity to individual needs and differences. Indeed, if a teacher is only interested in content, they may not serve the best interests of their students. Schussler et al. (2008) discusses case studies of 30 teacher candidates and how each of them fit into the domains previously mentioned: intellectual, cultural, and moral. Out of those 30 Schussler chose three teacher candidates, one that best exemplified each of the three domains. Lance was a preservice teacher who most identified with the intellectual domain. In identifying with the intellectual domain, he actually represented most of the 30 teacher candidates. Schussler states "Lance exemplifies a majority of the 30 teacher candidates by focusing on the pedagogical strategies that "solve" the problem for Jackie (one of Lance's students)" (p. 44). Most of these intellectual identifiers maintain that "staying true to their core discipline" is most important. But Schussler notes that "if Lance focuses primarily on making instructional decisions that "stay true to the core of English," he may make inappropriate curricular decisions that do not meet the needs of his individual students"(p. 48).

Smith, Hurst, and Skarbek (2005) describe "A Model for Defining the Construct of Caring in Teacher Education."

> There is a perception that the social and interpersonal aspects of teacher education are less important than content, technical, and instructional methods taught in teacher preparation and graduate programs. The inclusion of interpersonal and affective aspects in teacher education pedagogy may be prudent. Increasingly, many families depend on schools to act as an extension of their social support system, including emotional support and guidance for their children. (p. 27)

Glanz speaks to this topic also. In *Finding Your Leadership Style: A Guide for Educators* (2002) he states:

> These are the virtues and qualities that leaders should possess. However, most educational leadership programs emphasize the knowledge and skills considered necessary to function effectively as a leader. Witness the curriculum guidelines for advanced programs in educational leadership put out by the National Council for the Accreditation of Teacher Education (NCATE). The guidelines list leadership standards that describe the knowledge and skills candidates need to receive certification. Thus, too much focus is on knowledge, techniques, and methods. Policymakers are often afraid that educators cannot make good judgments in selecting and appointing those who have desirable intellectual, moral, and personal qualities, therefore they may resort to requiring what they consider observable and measurable behaviors.
>
> Leadership, then, is assessed merely by the possession of information and skills. Yet careful observation reveals that leaders are successful because their qualities (capacities) are well matched to the leadership position they

occupy, and because they exemplify special and necessary dispositions or virtues unique to education leaders. These virtues, although definable and identifiable, are not easily quantified or measured. Hence, in the selection of educational leaders, these virtues are usually overlooked. (pp. 10-11).

As mentioned in my book *The Unfinished Quest; the Plight of Progressive Science Education in the Age of Standards* (Berube, 2008), we are so committed to measuring outcomes (most of the time to satisfy arbitrary educational "standards") that we are losing sight of what is really important. It is *easy* to degrade something that we don't understand to a lowest common denominator, so that it can be easily measured and turned into a formula. What is hard, (and therefore at a higher level) is to be comfortable with those qualities that defy measurement to some degree, and most times these qualities are the ones that make a difference.

How do teachers *teach* for intelligence? In other words, how can teachers teach in such a way that their students not only know more information than they did before they took this teacher's class, but that the students themselves are now more intelligent as a result of this teacher? Robert Sternberg (2009) suggests that teachers teach analytically, which means to take something that is whole and to separate it into its constituent elements.

In 1956, Benjamin Bloom developed a classification system that still stands up today, whereby intellectual behavior important to learning was separated into three domains: cognitive, psychomotor, and affective. The cognitive domain was further divided into six levels, which demonstrate different intellectual skills. These go from the lowest levels of learning to the highest. (Verb examples are included that represent measurable intellectual activity, thereby letting the teacher know that the student knows).

1. Knowledge (lowest level) arrange, define, duplicate, label, list, memorize, name, order, recognize, relate, recall, repeat, reproduce;
2. Comprehension: classify, describe, discuss, explain, express, identify, indicate, locate, recognize, report, restate, review, select, translate;
3. Application: apply, choose, demonstrate, dramatize, employ, illustrate, interpret, operate, practice, schedule, sketch, solve, use, write;
4. Analysis: analyze, appraise, calculate, categorize, compare, contrast, criticize, differentiate, discriminate, distinguish, examine, experiment, question, test;

5. Synthesis: arrange, assemble, collect, compose, construct, create, design, develop, formulate, manage, organize, plan, prepare, propose, set up, write; and

6. Evaluation: (highest level) appraise, argue, assess, attach, choose compare, defend estimate, judge, predict, rate, core, select, support, value, evaluate (Bloom, 1956).

At the higher levels of the domain, we can see that analysis, synthesis and evaluation are where we get into higher level thinking skills. The first three (lower) levels of Bloom's taxonomy; knowledge, comprehension and application, are all necessary for creating well rounded students and are also necessary in order to move up to the higher levels in the domain. However, one can argue that you can memorize your way through these levels, without truly mastering the content or concept. In contract, beginning with analysis, a student is asked to now break down a concept into it's parts, a high level of cognitive activity, which leads to synthesizing (taking parts and creating a whole), and finally, evaluation, which is the highest levels of learning because it requires the student to be an expert on the content. Only experts on a topic can judge and critique it in depth.

In Robert Sternberg's article "Teaching for Wisdom, Intelligence, and Creativity" (2009) he asks:

> "How does one teach for wisdom, intelligence and creativity? Teaching analytically means encouraging students to (a) analyze, (b) critique, (c) judge, (d) compare and contrast, (e) evaluate and (f) assess. When teachers refer to teaching for critical thinking, they typically mean teaching for analytical thinking. A student could analyze a political argument critique a poem, judge the quality of a work of art, or compare and contrast two systems of government. Teaching creatively means encouraging students to (a) create, (b) invent, (c) discover, (d) imagine if …, (e) suppose that …, and (f) predict. Students could create a work of art, invent a machine that swims in the water, discover how force relates to mass, imagine what it would be like to grow up in a different culture, suppose that global temperatures keep increasing and speculate on the likely effects, or predict what will happen if the national debt keeps increasing at current rates. Teaching for creativity requires teachers not only to support and encourage creativity but also to model it and reward it when displayed. Unfortunately, this divergent way of teaching is not easily measurable. In other words, teachers need to not only talk the talk, but also to walk the walk. (p. 12)

Sternberg goes so far as to assess for intelligence using a measurement instrument that he developed, called the "Wisdom, Intelligence and Creativity, Synthesized," or WICS (2003). Indeed, Tufts University, where Sternberg is dean of arts and sciences, uses his instrument in their admission process, as a basis for admission. Sternberg says, "Here are actual essay topics we used for admissions to the Class of 2011. Completing the essays was optional":

- "The late scholar James O. Freedman referred to libraries as 'essential harbors on the voyage toward understanding ourselves.' What work of fiction or non-fiction would you include in your personal library? Why?" (Analytical)
- "Create a short story using one of the following topics: (a) The End of MTV; (b) Confessions of a Middle School Bully; (c) The Professor Disappeared; or (d) The Mysterious Lab" (Creative)
- "History's great events often turn on small moments. For example, what if Rosa Parks had given up her seat on that bus? What if Pope John Paul I had not died after a month in office in 1978? What if Gore had beaten Bush in Florida and won the 2000 U.S. presidential election? Using your knowledge of American or world history, choose a defining moment and imagine an alternate historical scenario if that key event had played out differently." (Creative)
- "Describe a moment in which you took a risk and achieved an unexpected goal. How did you persuade others to follow your lead? What lessons do you draw from this experience? You may reflect on examples from your academic, extracurricular or athletic experiences." (Practical)
- "A high school curriculum does not always afford much intellectual freedom. Describe one of your unsatisfied intellectual passions. How might you apply this interest to serve the common good and make a difference in society?" (Wisdom) (Sternberg, 2003, p. 14).

In *Outliers: The Story of Success*, Malcolm Gladwell (2008a) offers his opinion about intelligence, creativity, and teaching. In chapter 3, "The Trouble with Genius, Part 1," Gladwell points to other *factors* that people overlook when pondering intelligence, such as his discussion of the "threshold effect." With intelligence, there is a notion of being "smart enough," or what Gladwell calls the "threshold." He explains it this way:

Over the years, an enormous amount of research has been done in an attempt to determine how a person's performance on an IQ test ... translates to real-life success. People at the bottom of the scale—with an IQ below 70—are considered mentally disabled. A score of 100 is average; you probably need to be just above that mark to be able to handle college. To get into and succeed in a reasonably competitive graduate program, meanwhile, you probably need an IQ of at least 115. In general, the higher your score, the more education you'll get, the more money you're likely to make, and-believe it or not—the longer you'll live.

But there's a catch. The relationship between success and IQ works only up to a point. Once someone has reached an IQ of somewhere around 120, having additional IQ points doesn't seem to translate into any measurable real-world advantage." (pp. 78, 79)

So it appears that once a certain intelligence level is achieved (like a certain height in basketball), smarter is not necessarily better.

Gladwell gives an example of this phenomenon in what's called a "divergence test." This test is in direct contrast to tests where there is one correct answer to each question, or convergent thinking. This test calls for creativity and requires imagination in order to come up with numerous possible solutions to one single question. Gladwell collected samples of responses to such tests and reported the results:

Here, for example are answers to the "uses of objects" test collected by Liam Hudson from a student named Poole at a top British high school:

(Brick). To use in smash-and-grab raids. To help hold a house together. To use in a game of Russian roulette if you want to keep fit at the same time (bricks at ten paces, turn and throw-no evasive action allowed). To hold the eiderdown on a bed tie a brick at each corner. As a breaker of empty Coca-Cola bottles.

(Blanket). To use on a bed. As a cover for illicit sex in the woods. As a tent. To make smoke signals with. As a sail for a boat, cart or sled. As a substitute for a towel. As a target for shooting practice for short-sighted people. As a thing to catch people jumping out a burning skyscrapers" (p. 87).

Now, contrast these answers with the ones below submitted by a student named Florence (who was a prodigy and had the highest IQ in the school).

(Brick). Building things, throwing.

(Blanket). Keeping warm, smothering fire, tying to trees and sleeping in (as a hammock), improvised stretcher"(p. 88). Now Florence's IQ is higher than Poole's, but what do we notice about the answers? What we notice is the flexibility of Poole's mind, compared to the relative rigidity of Florence's. Poole scored lower on the convergent admissions test than had Florence, yet Poole's answers show more creativity and imagination.

In another example of the less than perfect correlation between IQ and success, Gladwell introduces us to Chris Langan, who many consider the smartest man in America. Langan's IQ is impossible to measure, it's off the charts and much, much higher than Albert Einstein's (which Gladwell reports was 150). Yet, did you recognize Langan's name when I mentioned him? It's not likely. But what if I mention Robert Oppenheimer? Yes, we've all heard of him ... the physicist who led a team of scientists in the famous "Manhattan Project" during World War II.

These two men had equally well connected brains, but totally opposite circumstances. Langan was extremely poor and raised by a single mother. No one in Langan's family had a college education. Langan was so gifted that in high school, he was offered full scholarships to two colleges, and chose Reed over the University of Chicago. Unaware of how to work the college machine and with no guidance from home, he fumbled. Not with his classwork, which was stellar, but with the bureaucracy that everyone has to endure as a part of their college experiences; I like to call it "jumping through hoops." Langan was easily intimidated by his professors and administrators around campus and didn't know how to speak to them. After transferring to Montana State, things weren't much better. One day, after his transmission fell out of his car, he begged his advisor to switch him to afternoon classes. His advisor denied his request, ignorant of both the struggles he has already endured to get to where he was, but also of his great intelligence. Langan couldn't communicate in a way that conveyed his gifts, nor could he negotiate with those in positions of authority. So he quit school.

Let's look at Robert Oppenheimer now. He was as smart as Langan, but had parents that pampered his intellect and knew how to shepherd him through the educational system. He went to Harvard and then to Cambridge where he studied physics. A gifted tutor named Patrick Blackett (later a Nobel Prize winner) took him under his wing to show him the ropes. It was during this time though, that Oppenheimer became emotionally unstable, and actually took chemicals from his lab and tried to poison his tutor. So with attempted murder facing him, he was slapped on the wrist and given probation. Langan struggles with poverty, cars that fall apart; a mother that misses a financial aid deadline, lack of mentors, and a lost scholarship. Oppenheimer tries to murder his tutor, get's slapped on the back of the hand, and later winds up in charge of the most high-profile, dangerous project in World War II. Why? Because Langan didn't have what Gladwell calls "practical intelligence," and Oppenheimer did. Oppenheimer gave such a brilliant speech during his criminal defense, that he got the higher ups to see things his way. Practical intelligence is knowing what to say, how to say it, and when to say it. This is a factor (one of the "X" factors) in a person's success ... communication skills that advance your life and cause. (pp. 91-101)

CHAPTER 3

SELF-REFLECTION/VALUES

Thinking about thinking, or meta-cognition is an important part of teacher education. Teachers who employ self-reflection are better teachers. In chapter 1, I mentioned teacher dispositions and how important they are toward a successful teaching career. But again, the problem with them is that they are hard to quantify. It is only through behavioral analysis can we "observe" teacher dispositions at work. That is why it is so important during the teacher preparation process for preservice teachers to think about who and where they are in the universe called schooling. Self-directed reflection is vital if teachers want to truly understand their students. With the vast majority of American teachers coming from the middle-class mentality, including members all races, then if we don't realize that we are looking at our students as if we are superior to them, we are not respecting them.

Schussler, Bercaw, and Stooksberry (2008) presented to preservice teachers case studies of situations that could occur in a classroom, in order to measure their dispositions. They found that they could indeed uncover each preservice teacher's dispositions by asking the teacher candidates to self-reflect in their analysis of each case. "Because there is a paucity of empirical research examining the development of dispositions and because we wanted a thick description of candidate thinking, we employed a qualitative design that highlighted three candidates" (p. 41). One such student, "Margaret," was forced to examine her prejudices about the children in the class through this exercise. Margaret was shown

The "X" Factor: Personality Traits of Exceptional Science Teachers
pp. 27–30
Copyright © 2010 by Information Age Publishing

to have problems in the cultural domain of her students. She assumed that the students' home lives were "lacking" in some way, therefore Margaret is of the opinion that the teacher in this case study, Jackie, should attempt to "fill in" what is "missing." "Margaret fails to acknowledge that Jackie possesses a culture that influences her understanding of her students. Furthermore, Margaret fails to recognize that she herself possesses a culture that affects how she views the case" (p. 45). This exercise forced Margaret to deal with her unconscious biases.

> Margaret's unfounded assumptions that students had uncaring parents and would not graduate could result in detrimental instructional decisions if she does not develop greater awareness within the cultural domain. Despite her inclination to establish caring relationships with her students (moral domain), and her knowledge of instructional strategies (intellectual domain), Margaret may fall short of accomplishing her goals if she does not move beyond a superficial awareness of diversity (cultural domain). (p. 48)

Another preservice student, "Ally," was also asked to critique Jackie's case study. According to Ally: Jackie has a different background than her students. What Jackie doesn't realize is that her students may be very happy in their lives, even if they chose not to go to college. "Jackie needs to think about how to reach her students but she needs to realize that she can't do that if she goes in thinking she is … better than them"(Schusser et al., p. 46). So we see that Margaret doesn't "get it" as well as Ally does. Ally acknowledges that teachers and students hold different worldviews and values. "By articulating that what might be considered desirable to one person (i.e., attending college) may not lead to a happy life for another, Ally demonstrates awareness within the moral domain that few teacher candidates in this study expressed" (p. 46). Where Margaret sees differences as deficits, Ally just sees differences. One of the values Ally believes in is that "despite being educated herself, she believes that a teacher must not dictate a student's worldview and value system"(p. 47).

One of the benefits of self-reflection is that a person can discover what their values are. It is amazing how many people can't describe their value systems. These values that we have in turn, dictate no less than how we view the world. Self-reflection uncovers for us, our biases, worldviews and assumptions. A person who has never reflected on his or her life, believes that their way of viewing the world may be the only logical and correct way of viewing it. This can be a recipe for disaster if a middle class teacher is put in charge of teaching lower socioeconomic status students. The reverse may also be true. Middle class teachers who walk into a privileged private school may have assumptions about the students that are also incorrect, thereby negatively affecting their instruction. Schussler et al. cites another study (Banks, Cochran-Smith, Moll, Richert, Zeichner, and

LePage, 2005). "According to Banks et al. (2005), 'teachers need to know how to examine their own cultural assumptions to understand how these shape their starting points for practice' ... and later 'undoing prior assumptions is an important part of this process of learning to teach children who are not one's own'" (p. 48).

The data from Schussler et al.'s study "suggest an inverse relationship between awareness and assumptions. The most potentially egregious assumptions were most likely to occur with the teacher candidates who possessed the least amount of awareness in a domain" (p. 48). This lack of awareness stems from a lack of self-reflection.

Value-driven education has taken on a different meaning than it originally had. John Dewey, the progressive philosopher who left a massive footprint on American education, had dreams of how the proper education of children would lead to better citizens of the world by producing problem solvers, and better thinkers. M. Berube (2000) says;

> for Dewey, thinking begins in what fairly enough may be called a forked-road situation. In his classic statement on thinking, *How We Think*, Dewey proposed a process that occurs when thinking: (1) a "suggestion ... to a possible solution"; (2) "an intellectualization of the difficulty that has been *felt* (directly experienced) into a *problem* to be solved"; a *hypothesis*, to initiate and guide observation and other operations in collection of factual material"; and "testing the hypothesis by overt or imaginative action." (p. 41)

Dewey was also intensely interested in moral education.

> After nurturing intellectual abilities, Dewey argued "the development of character is the end of all school work." Indeed, in the greatly expanded revision (of *How We Think*), Dewey entitled one section "The Problem of Training Thought" and another "Why Reflective Thinking Must Be an Educational Aim" ... Dewey wanted teachers to see that "moral ideals ... be realized in persons." He proposed a "moral trinity of the school ... of social intelligence, social power, and social interests." In short, Dewey equated moral values with a social consciousness aimed at restructuring society. In this sense, the "moral responsibility of the school ... is to society ... (since) ... the school has the power to modify the social order." (p. 41)

So we see that a self-reflective, morally responsible school experience, is at the heart of nothing less than democracy itself. Teachers who possess a personality that allows for self-reflection and self-observation, are better teachers, and in turn, create better citizens.

Unfortunately, in today's climate, too often morals and values are often connected with strict religious dogma, to the point of completely betraying the very roots of why Dewey thought values and moral ideals were important enough to teach to our students; so as to ensure the continuation and future of our free democracy, and the freedoms we enjoy, including freedom of and/or from religion in public schools. When we hear of "values-driven education" nowadays, it is in an attempt to mold curriculum and school culture into a set of strict religious rules. To prove how ridiculous this has become, think of the word "social." The word use to have a positive connotation, where we thought of our fellow human beings and their welfare. Now it is used by many conservatives to insinuate a socialistic drive towards education, using social justice issues to pollute the meaning of the phrase. Democratic education was *created* on the very platform of social justice issues, to unite the poor and the rich in the American classroom, which would in turn, level the playing field for opportunity. This notion alone is why it is so vital to improve public education in America, rather than running from it when problems arise. It is truly the last best democratic institution in America.

CHAPTER 4

AFFECTION AND CARING

What is the big deal if a teacher doesn't have "affection" for his or her students? Smith and Emigh (2005) think it is a big deal. It is no secret, as mentioned earlier in this book, that the current educational climate cares more about measuring outcomes than it does teacher/student relationships. *How* a student feels is less important than *what* she knows. "Caring, in contrast to the technical dimensions of teaching, gives priority to relationships and how these relationships are socially constructed" (p. 27). As to why there is little importance afforded to caring in the classroom, "There are several possibilities that may explain reasons why content regarding the social interaction aspects of schools has been diminished recently in teacher education. First, there has been a quest for efficiency of instructional method, most notably characterized by time on task. This emphasis on maximizing the on-task behaviors and orientation of teachers has sent a message to teacher educators that spending instruction time in building relationships has little value in education—concurrently, and most recently, there has been political and societal pressure to produce acceptable scores in high-stakes assessment programs. As such, inquiry activities in educational settings to document and research social or relational aspects in students have been depreciated and neglected" (p. 28).

What exactly is a "caring behavior"? According to Smith and Emigh, the first component is "an ability to attend to academic, social, and emotional areas of students" (p. 31). Like self-reflection and values, Dewey

The "X" Factor: Personality Traits of Exceptional Science Teachers
pp. 31–34
Copyright © 2010 by Information Age Publishing

also left his imprint in this domain. Caring behavior sounds a lot like John Dewey's notions of what schooling should be all about, the *whole* child, and the very building blocks of progressive education. Dewey has been called the "father of American Education" for good reason. He practically spearheaded the whole progressive education movement with his views that schools and civil society should be different sides of the same coin. M. Berube, in his book *Eminent Educators* (2000), describes Dewey as "a philosopher, educator, and social activist whose thinking revolutionized American education" (p. 34).

> Dewey's approach to education was renaissance in scope. Dewey's philosophy of education encompassed what he considered the "whole child," that is, the development of intellectual, moral, social and artistic abilities of the child. Learning was not a genetically fixed operation but was essentially process oriented and significantly responsive to schooling." (p. 40)

M. Berube also notes "Under girding Dewey's philosophy of education was a strong moral component. After nurturing intellectual abilities, Dewey argues 'the development of character is the end of all school work' " (p. 41).

Another version of what caring might look like has been called "culturally responsive" behavior. With most of our schools now housing students from all walks of life, both racially, culturally, socially and ability wise, it seems that the age of the homogeneous classroom is a thing of the past. But have we as educators caught up with this trend? Even in terms of boys and girls, do we know as teachers how they think alike? Differently? We don't view sex of a student as a diversity issue, since everyone is either male or female, but there are differences in how the sexes view the world, which can effect how they are educated. Content area is one thing, placing that content (math, English) into context, is another. Learning about differences (some may say *details*), show students we care about them enough to make the effort. And in the end, we are also learning things about ourselves as teachers, too.

Carol Gilligan, professor at New York University and formerly of Harvard, has done seminal work in bringing to light some of these differences between boys and girls. In 1982, Gilligan wrote a book entitled *In A Different Voice: Psychological Theory and Women's Development*, that changed the way we view morality and gender in terms of how differently boys and girls view relational problems and situations that call for conflict resolution. Gilligan had been mentored under Lawrence Kohlberg during her grad school experiences at Harvard University, working toward a PhD in social psychology. During this time, she noticed that the research involved mostly male subjects, as if the women's point of view was not valid. She began to conduct research on morality and gender, and the notion of selfishness and selflessness. When Gilligan began to interview girls, she noticed that they underwent a loss of self-esteem at about the time of puberty, where they had previously been self-assured, confident, and outspoken little girls. Upon further investigation, Gilligan uncovered the phenomenon she named "losing your voice," which she penned to describe what adolescent girls were metaphorically experiencing. One can "see" this in science classrooms all over America, where young girls muzzle themselves for fear of loss of self-esteem in front of their peers, or for not wanting to appear smarter then the boy sitting next to her that she wants to date.

Gilligan at this time coined the terms "ethic of justice" and "ethic of care" to describe the framework through which the sexes made sense of the world. This can best be described by Gilligan's use of "the Heinz dilemma" in *In A Different Voice*, where she interviews both boys and girls to uncover their opinions on a moral issue.

> In this particular dilemma, a man named Heinz considers whether or not to steal a drug which he cannot afford to buy in order to save the life of his wife. In the standard format of Kohlberg's interviewing procedure, the description of the dilemma itself-Heinz's predicament, the wife's disease, the druggist's refusal to lower his price-is followed by the question, "Should Heinz steal the drug?" The reasons for and against stealing are then explored through a series of questions that vary and extend the parameters of the dilemma in a way designed to reveal the underlying structure of moral thought. (p. 26)

Her findings are very revealing. What Gilligan uncovered was that boys saw justice and logic in the answers to the dilemma. Boys said absolutely not, that Heinz should not steal the drug, and if he does, he should go to jail in order to preserve social order. The girls saw the solution more in terms of maintaining relationships, and even suggested bartering of services as a way to resolve the problem without any laws being broken. The girls see the gray area of morality, and the bigger picture. To the boys, it was very black and white; a mathematical problem with a logical solution. Girls were working from an ethic of care, and boys from an ethic of justice. Boys thought of the problems in linear terms, and tended to think in terms of black/white issues, in terms of right and wrong. Girls tended to be more flexible in their thinking, more circular, in that they figured out ways of bartering with Heinz, where no relationships would be sacrificed (with the druggist) and where they would still get what they wanted. Relationships mattered to the girls. This basic blueprint from which the sexes view the world, has a huge influence on learning and classroom experience.

How can today's schoolteachers incorporate this ethic of care into their curricula? Especially in this culturally diverse society? Garza (2009) examined Latino and White high school students' perceptions of teacher behaviors that convey caring. Findings of the students' perceptions uncovered five major themes: (a) provide scaffolding during a teaching episode, (b) reflect a kind disposition through actions, (c) are always available to the student, (d) show a personal interest in the student's well-being inside and outside the classroom, (e) and provide affective academic support in the classroom setting. Garza states:

> providing preservice teachers with concrete examples of what secondary students view as critical to fostering relationships and a sense of belonging can only enhance their pedagogical knowledge and skills and understanding about high school students' needs. Also, cooperating teachers, supervising teachers, university supervisors, and other individuals who mentor ethnically unique adolescents and student teachers could use these findings as a way to enhance relationships and improve communication. The notion that culture may affect students' perceptions of caring behaviors merits further examination to determine whether culturally and linguistically unique middle school, high school, and postsecondary students have the same points of view. (p. 318)

We see from the experts, that you cannot separate dispositions from personality. Nor can you be an effective teacher without proper self-reflection and attention to what values you hold that may or may not be influencing the students in your classroom. We will see now, in chapter 5, how important it is to have caring teachers.

PART II

WHAT MATTERS

CHAPTER 5

OUR FAVORITE TEACHERS

Whenever I look back on my life, I realize that my greatest role models have always been teachers, whether they were grade-school teachers or college professors. The parenting skills I most admired in my step-father Teddy were his leadership skills, in the truest sense of the word. He taught my siblings and me so many things, mostly about life and how to navigate it successfully. He taught us things that no one else did, and I look back now in amazement and wonder as to what might have become of us if he had not married my mother. To this very day, as I teach my college classes, I frequently hear Teddy's words coming from my own mouth, as I try to lead my students into adulthood.

Teddy only had a high school diploma, though he was very intelligent. He grew up on the Eastern Shore of Virginia, and moved to Norfolk, Virginia when he was 8 or 9. He was a rascal of the first order, prompting the principal and vice principal of his high school to corner him at the local pool hall and drag him back to school on many occasions. The principal would approach him from the front door, and the vice principal would cover the back exit as he tried to escape. But as he grew into manhood, he showed great intellectual curiosity. People loved him. Teddy had the best people skills of anyone I have ever known, period. He has always been compared to Rhett Butler (or Clark Gable's take on Rhett Butler). And he loved his "children" as if we were his own. There was no "step" allowed in our house, he was our Dad and we were his kids, plain and simple. He was extremely charming. It was wonderful to be his daughter. I would watch

The "X" Factor: Personality Traits of Exceptional Science Teachers
pp. 37–57

him work his magic on people from all walks of life, and he treated all equally. He taught us about extending dignity to people of all races and stations in life. I truly learned how to exist in the world with people from watching him.

Probably the thing I admire most about him was his ability to cheer me on, to truly be my best fan as I earned my degrees. Although he had no college degree himself, he was very proud of me. We would regularly discuss the latest thing I was studying, especially in science classes, as we both loved science and physics. We would sit at the pub together and draw on paper napkins whatever I had been studying on string theory or black holes. He would remark that as long as we could discuss everything I was learning, he was getting almost two degrees for the price of one! I remember 2 weeks after I began my doctoral studies, being told that he would go to his favorite pub around the time I would appear on the local television channel as I taught my televised course as a grad assistant, and proudly cluck and brag to his buddies as he forced them to change the channel from sports to my broadcast. Very shortly after that, he died suddenly of a massive brain-stem stroke. My main support and cheerleader in academia was now gone, and I was faced with forging along without him. He would not be there 4-years later as I earned my doctorate during my graduation ceremony, but at least he saw me begin my PhD studies. He was always in my corner. My greatest academic supporter had barely a high school diploma. No major academic content ever passed between us, unless it was from me to him. Yet, he was *my* favorite teacher.

Sometimes we have teachers that we remember with mixed emotions. I had a "real" teacher whom I will never forget. Her name was Ms. H, who I had for a forth-grade teacher at Arrowhead Elementary in Virginia Beach. Ms. H was a history buff, and would dress up as the characters in history, switching back and forth with costumes as she narrated historical events, like the Boston Tea Party, or when American Indians roamed the very place where our school now sat. We would venture outside to look for arrowheads, which had been found where our school was built, hence the name. She would also let us take breaks during the day. If we were getting antsy during math for instance, she would pick up on this and would say "everybody up" and we would pop up from our desks to get ready for a game of yarn ball toss. We had to put one arm behind our backs, while we threw a yarn ball around the room, jumping, straining to catch it with one hand, while our technique suffered from being doubled over with laughter.

We would also once in a while play "mud soccer" during recess. We would always have a spare set of clothes at school for this game. We would go out after a good rain, and play soccer in the mud for the whole hour of recess or physical education. We got really muddy and dirty, but we had a blast. Unfortunately, I can't imagine modern teachers allowing students to play in the mud, but these are things you never forget.

Even though Ms. H was my favorite elementary school teacher, people can be complicated. She did humiliate me once in the hallway, probably not intending to. My parents had been divorced since I was in the first grade, and I can't remember what stresses we were going through at home during my fourth-grade year, but I must have done something during school that day to upset her. In the hallway after school, she came up to me, grabbed me by the shoulders, looked me in the eye, and said loudly "Clair … what's wrong with you?" This was not said in a sympathetic way, but in an angry, derogatory way that stuck with me for a long time, and that made me wonder "is there something wrong with me?" Even our favorite teachers can be complex and can leave us with mixed experiences, most great, some painful. But that event always prevented me from holding Ms. Hoover completely up on a pedestal, like a favorite teacher should be. But one of the benefits of being in a special teacher's class is that you tend to remember most of your classmates in that class too. Teachers who make for memorable classes enable their students to remember most everything about that class, including classmates. Many of us from Ms. H's fourth grade class keep in touch, and we all still have fond memories of her and of each other.

In college, I had a handful of professors that I really enjoyed, including Dr. Gordon Magnuson, a funny English professor, Drs. Donald Wolfgang and Barry Lipscomb, very caring and empathetic psychology professors (who influenced me to get my first undergraduate degree in psychology), Dr. Rebecca Bowers, a science education professor who took me under her wing, showed me the ropes of academia, and recruited me into the doctoral program, and Dr. Jim Heinen, the funniest statistics professor of all time. (I laughed more in his statistics class than is normal for statistics I'm sure!) Heinen was hysterical, but he taught me statistics, and for a math phobic person, he worked miracles and changed the way I thought about myself. He also made me realize that a person can go through his or her whole life *believing* that they can't learn something, which in turn affects their decisions about what to take in school, or what career path to embark upon. This made a lasting impression as I set out to teach future teachers.

I have compiled here some narratives of some of our favorite teachers. Some of these people you might know, others may be unknown to you. But they all share their insights and give us clues as to what makes a teacher special and unique. Let's first hear what they have to say, and then I will share with you some patterns and clues I have found in their narratives that will shed light on what makes a teacher truly great.

HOWARD GARDNER

Dr. Gardner is the John H. and Elisabeth A. Hobbs Professor of Cognition and Education at Harvard's Graduate School of Education. Although he has amassed a huge and important vita, he is famous mostly for his "Theory of Multiple Intelligences" which has been widely acknowledged since its publication in 1993 as one of the best ways to account for individual differences in children in our classrooms by redefining what intelligence actually is. Dr. Gardner's childhood was influenced by two tragic events, the death of his brother (before Howard was born) and his family's loss in the Holocaust; both events having been shoved under the rug and hidden from little Howard. Gardner places his family as his biggest influence in his life, both then and now with his wife, children, and grandchildren.

Gardner doesn't use the language of "favorite teachers," but instead "most influential" to his life and career. These include psychologists Jerome Bruner, philosopher Nelson Goodman, and neurologist Norman Geschwind. He met these gentlemen in the 1960s and he credits them with transforming his intellectual development at that time. Gardner has made the important connection between personality traits (nonintellectual factors) and temperament to creative achievement.

Gardner's mother Hilde, an escapee from Nazi Germany, is certainly one of his favorite teachers. She diligently sat beside him every day for years as he practiced the piano. She was also involved in other aspects of scouting, schooling, and other activities that showed Howard and his sister Marion that they *mattered* and were *important*. He notes that he liked his teachers but was rarely "stretched" by them. The greatest intellectual influence in Howard Gardner's life was the Swiss psychologist Jean Piaget, whom he had the honor of meeting a few times. (Gardner told me once that he saw Piaget right before Gardner was to be married, and that he felt that Piaget "blessed" the union!) Piaget's work became the springboard off of which Gardner fashioned his career. Gardner disagreed with Piaget on several issues, but this did not quell the respect and affection he had for Piaget, as Gardner tried to take Piaget's work to a higher, more complex and nuanced level. So as Piaget once "grew" Gardner's mind, Gardner now sought to "grow" Piaget.

If you were to ask Dr. Gardner what makes for a good teacher, he would tell you that successful teaching must grapple with a student's current level of understanding or misunderstanding of the topic you are teaching. Many students have attractive, but false notions and it is the teacher's responsibility to challenge these misconceptions and help students arrive at more veridical models of the world. I have also gathered from Dr. Gardner that if you make a student feel that they matter and are important, they will never forget it and will strive to live up to your expectations, as he did with his mother. Gardner's favorite teachers didn't just teach him new content that he did not know previously, they *changed* him forever. They *changed* his mind. They challenged, moved, and rearranged his world so that he could move up the ladder of sophistication in his own intellectual life. Indeed, one of a teacher's main jobs is as a "mind-changer" for their students. Teachers also should challenge. The definition of the word "challenge" includes to dispute, to question, to confront, to call out, and to compete. A good teacher is actually a "disruptive" force in a child's life in this way. And Dr. Gardner knows this is a good thing, in fact, it's what education is all about (Dr. Howard Gardner, personal communication, January 28, 2009; Shaler & Gardner, 2007).

NEIL DEGRASSE TYSON

Dr. Neil deGrasse Tyson is an astrophysicist and the director of the Hayden Planetarium in New York City, and the host of the PBS show *NOVA Science NOW*. He is regarded as one of the most popular and well-known physicists in the world. I recently spoke with Dr. Tyson about his favorite and most influential teachers, where he generously gave me a half hour to talk with him. I also met him after a presentation at the 2009 World Science Festival in New York City, but more one that later.

Dr. Tyson first fell in love with science when he was 9 years old, after a visit (appropriately enough) to the Hayden Planetarium in New York with his family. Tyson describes his personal learning preferences as visual, he was a good reader and learned more on his own almost than he did in class. His parents were not scientists, however, his father was a sociologist who had worked for Mayor John Lindsay, and his mother was a housewife. When asked about his favorite teachers of all time, he mentioned Mr. Russell, his seventh-grade social studies teacher. Dr. Tyson recalls that Mr. Russell was a great expressive storyteller with awesome verbal abilities, and showed enthusiasm and passion for his subject, which he knew quite well, having a vast knowledge of its content. He was articulate and clear with expectations, but was a tough grader. Tyson notes that there was no "distance" between he and his students, meaning that Mr. Russell did not use power as a tool for control. He was always available for his students with very little formality.

Another role model was Mark Chartrand, the director of the Hayden Planetarium in the 1970s. Tyson described Chartrand as brilliant, witty and funny, with a strong pedagogical sensibility. Chartrand was Dr. Tyson's academic and scientific role model during that time. There was also Fred Hess, an instructor at Hayden, who gave live shows and taught courses on the night sky, which Tyson remembers fondly as being the reason he fell in love with the night sky in this childhood. Tyson said that Hess conveyed a "romance" and love for science that was contagious.

I asked Dr. Tyson how important he thinks good verbal skills are for science and mathematics professors, in other words, as long as they are experts in content, does it matter how it is delivered? "Well, it depends" responded Tyson. He was referring to undergraduate versus graduate students. At the graduate level, the communication skills of the professor are really irrelevant. These professors are mostly helping grad students in physics or mathematics with extremely high level content, and mentoring them in their own (students') research. These students *know* the material, they are insanely internally *driven*, and they don't need a professor skilled at storytelling to hook them to science. Graduate students are *already scientists* themselves; they mainly need guidance and mentoring. On the other hand, it absolutely matters if you are teaching undergrad students physics courses. Tyson said that at the undergraduate level, a good professor in the math or science fields needs to communicate clearly with his or her students, not just to lecture. The professor also has to know her audience, and know the barriers to communication between herself and her undergraduate students.

Tyson stressed this point again and again. Knowing the demographics of your students is vital, and he said that all good professors of undergraduate students should have what he called a "cultural/social utility belt" loaded with tools and techniques aimed at communicating the proper content in the right way to a certain group. Tyson also made this distinction in terms of the general public. Giving a lecture to the general public on physics topics is very much like teaching undergraduate students. Giving a talk to a group of fellow scientists, however, is quite another thing.

Successful teachers know how to teach in ways that grabs students' attention, and makes them want to learn more. There is a technique by which to do this, and it is called "top-down" or "conceptual" teaching. I spoke of this method in an article I wrote in 2000 called "A Conceptual Model for Middle School Science Instruction" (Berube, 2000). Dr. Tyson mentioned this top-down approach also, where you teach big concepts first, then the mathematical details later. If a student learns concepts and how they are related to each other, then they don't have to memorize nearly as much content. Here's how I described it:

> "Picture a middle school science classroom. The students memorize the speed of light and then use this information to convert energy into mass by employing the formula $E = MC^2$. The students forget the memorized information, however, before the red ink on the returned test is dry. Suppose instead that seventh graders were taught Einstein's theory of relativity as a concept before the first formula were taught. Suppose also that only after

the students understood the theory conceptually would they then be considered ready to learn the formulas necessary for experimentation and replication. And, having first learned general relativity conceptually, they would then be introduced to related concepts, such as the big bang theory, black holes, quantum gravity, the red shift of light, time travel, and Einstein's famous hypothetical twin paradox.

Linear Versus Conceptual Learning

We live in a linear-thinking world, filled with linear-thinking teachers who teach in a linear way. However, much of science is not linear. Theoretical ideas do not always follow rational step-by-step construction and often occur by apparently "skipping" so-called logical, normal steps (call them quantum leaps, if you will). Current research supports the advantages of conceptual learning over memorization. Bruce Albert (Carey, 1997), president of the National Academy of Sciences and a former biochemistry teacher of medical students at the University of California at San Francisco, is disheartened by the fact that his students "parroted back biochemical terms but failed to grasp the concepts ... [and] were not really learning anything" (p. 66). Albert blames standardized multiple choice tests, claiming that they "emphasize memorization and word association over conceptual knowledge ... [and are] poor judges of students' abilities" (p. 66). The result, according to Albert, is a generation of students bereft of the analytical skills needed to be successful science students and basically turned off by science. (p. 312)

Another trait that Dr. Tyson felt was important for a teacher to have is humor. In his words, "the professor has to *want* them (the students) to *want* to be there." There is no better way to hook students to any content, than through humor. Charisma and charm were not so high on Dr. Tyson's list, but he did say that the subject that you are teaching should be made charming if at all possible, and humor is the best way to achieve that (N. deGrasse Tyson, personal communication, March 17, 2009).

Dr. Tyson agrees with me that this is the way to go when teaching elementary, middle, high school, and undergraduate college students. On what makes for great teachers, it is ultimately up to the teacher to get the content through to the student. Even today, when Tyson teaches his college classes, he accepts the burden of the professor, and blames himself if the students aren't getting it. So he will adjust his strategy until they do get it. I agree that this is a great quality to have. He said that passion and enthusiasm are infectious, and that even though a teacher has to be a content expert, it is *equally important* for the teacher to have this enthusiasm and passion for the topic since this is what is ultimately passed on to students.

MALCOLM GLADWELL

Malcolm Gladwell has written some of my favorite books, including *Outliers: The Story of Success* (2008a), *Blink* (2005) and *The Tipping Point: How Little Things Can Make a Big Difference* (2000). Born in 1963 in England and raised in Canada, Gladwell currently lives in New York City and is a staff writer for *The New Yorker*. Born of a Jamaican mother and British father, Gladwell is fascinated with human social behavior, and writes brilliantly about it in his books, including the notion of "charisma" in *The Tipping Point* that I have used in this book to make connections to education.

Malcolm Gladwell is an interesting looking fellow, the sort of a person that you would cross a room to want to speak to. He is articulate, intelligent, and has a quality that I greatly admire, which is the ability to connect various seemingly unrelated phenomena and to put them together in new ways no one has ever thought to before. He has a gift for synthesis. (I admire this trait more than criticism, because I feel that it is more of a creative endeavor where new thought forms are born).

Education is extremely important in Gladwell's family. His father is a civil-engineering professor at the University of Waterloo, his mother is a psychotherapist and book author, and a role model for Malcolm's as a writer. He was named by *Time* magazine in 2005 as one of its 100 most influential people. Each of his three books has landed on the *New York Times* best seller list. Gladwell's brother is an elementary school principal. I talk more about his brother in this book concerning what it takes to become a "star" teacher." I was very eager to hear what Gladwell had to say about his favorite teacher, since he was one of the inspirations for me to write this book, and he was very gracious to contact me with this contribution.

Gladwell's favorite teacher was a seventh-grade teacher named Jim DeBock. He remembers what he looked like and what kind of car he drove: "He was very tall and had a long bushy red beard and drove an aging Triumph TR4 sports car." (I think that it is interesting that when we really like a teacher, we notice things about them that have nothing to do with teaching ... we are in effect noticing the "whole person," or "essence" of the teacher). Mr. DeBock incorporated his love for writing by requiring his students to keep a daily journal where they would write a story a day, very useful no doubt to this budding writer. Mr. DeBock also insisted upon respect for each other in his classroom. What about Mr. DeBock's expertise in whatever subject matter he taught? Here's what Gladwell has to say:

> I met him as an adult, years later, and was struck by how eccentric he was, in the best possible way. He was kind of a hippie holdover, fond of saying

slightly strange and quirky things. I also realized how charismatic he is. He was a kind of pied piper. I don't think all teachers need to be that charismatic. And I can't even tell you whether, technically speaking, he was a good teacher. But he had a profound impact on me, because he made me realize that your imagination was a muscle, and if you exercised it regularly and took it seriously, you could accomplish great things. I think about him all the time." This is about as great a testament to any teacher you can give. He never really told me what he even taught! But he left a lasting impression (M. Gladwell, personal communication, March 3, 2009).

DIANE RAVITCH

Diane Ravitch was born in Houston Texas, the product of Houston public schools. She is a graduate of Wellesley College and Columbia University, and currently lives in Brooklyn, New York.

I had the pleasure of first meeting Diane Ravitch, one of the leading historians of American education, several years ago while my husband (M. Berube) was writing his book *Eminent Educators: Studies in Intellectual Influence* (Greenwood Press, 2002). Dr. Ravitch was one of the persons to be highlighted in the book. We met her in her office at New York University, where she is a research professor of education. She is also a senior fellow at the Hoover Institute at Stanford University, and the Brookings Institution in Washington, DC. Ravitch was also the assistant secretary of education and counselor to Lamar Alexander during the G.H.W. Bush administration. Dr. Ravitch is quiet, soft spoken, and hugely intelligent. Her quiet demeanor belies her fiery passion for education, and her strong sense of service as a public intellectual, often taking on the powers that be in the *New York Times* and other publications. Dr. Ravitch possesses the unique quality of being soft and quiet, and at the same time outspoken. She has become a friend to my husband and a great source of educational wisdom and encouragement for me.

During a recent personal communication (January 28, 2009), Dr. Ravitch spoke of her favorite teacher. The one she remembers best as the most influential, was a homeroom teacher of Ravitch's at San Jacinto High School in Houston, named Ruby Ratliff. Mrs. Ratliff taught English literature where Ravitch would find herself as a senior in high school.

Mrs. Ratliff was gruff and demanding. She had high expectations. She did not tolerate foolishness or disruptions. Her manner tended to attract kids like me, who wanted a demanding teacher like her. However, her classes always had a wide range of students, as our school had no ability tracking and no gifted classes. What I remember most about her was what she taught us. We were exposed to the greatest writers of the English language, not in long writings like novels, but in poems, essays, and even a play or two. We read Shakespeare, Keats, Shelley, Wordsworth, Milton, and other great English writers.

Ravitch was obviously a great student, and one who sought out challenging teachers. But most students also feel that teachers shouldn't teach down to them, that teachers should push them to do their best. This is mentioned by Ravitch who said

> Mrs. Ratliff did nothing for our "self-esteem" other than challenge us to meet her exacting standards. I always thought that she saw herself bringing enlightenment to barbarians (that was us). She insisted that our writing had to be correct. When you wrote something for her class, you were very careful about spelling, grammar and syntax. Otherwise, it would be returned to you with red marks. She was always sure to make a comment that encouraged you to do a better job.

I've mentioned content throughout this book. I believe in content … strong, high-level expertise in your subject area. So I was curious to see where Mrs. Ratliff fell in this spectrum.

> It was clear to me that she (Mrs. Ratliff) loved her subject and loved the respect that the students showed her, especially since this was a large high school where students did not easily give respect to their teachers. Many years after I finished high school, I tracked down Mrs. Ratliff to thank her for what she had done for me. I located her in a nursing home in South Carolina. We corresponded off and on, and we had a few phone conversations. In one of then, I was going on about how wonderful it was to study literature with her and she started laughing! I asked her why she was laughing and she said that she was *teaching out of license. She was actually certified to teach social studies!*"

Mrs. Ratliff would not have lasted a minute in today's classrooms with our standards movement. This is unfortunate in my opinion. Ravitch said of standards:

> I question whether there really is a national standards movement, since there are zero standards in any subject; the reading and math tests in many states are dumbed down, and there are no standards in history, English, science, etc. In most places, teachers are teaching to the tests, which are not very good tests.

I couldn't agree more on all points.

The national standards movement has been severely under funded, hence the cheap and ubiquitous bubble tests. Now with a new administration there is a hope that more funds will be available in order to carry out the mission of measuring standards properly. One of the things that needs to be addressed is that there are enthusiastic, passionate teachers who know a great deal about a certain subject, or may even be an expert, but are not formally certified to teach it. I am not placing a value judgment here one way or the other, but this begs questions in this era of huge teacher shortages. Could we offer "content" testing in certain areas, where prospective teachers could "test out" of certain classes they would need for regular certification? It seems a shame that if Dr. Ravitch was a student in today's classroom, there would be no Mrs. Ratliff there to teach her English. Social studies, yes, but not English.

"At graduation, she gave a line or two of poetry to each of the members of her homeroom as a graduation present. I got these two:

'To strive, to seek, to find, and not to yield. To strive, to seek, to find, and not to yield' which was the last line of Tennyson's 'Ulysses.' which we had read in class. And 'among them, but not of them,' from Byron's 'Childe Harold's Pilgrimage,' which we had not read in class. I think these were the best graduation presents I got, because they the only ones that I remember fifty years later! I can't tell you that she made me what I am today; why blame my English teacher? But I can say that she is the teacher that I remember best today." (D. Ravitch, personal communication, January 28, 2009)

JEFFREY GLANZ

One of the best and brightest leaders in academia in the New York City area, or indeed the entire country, is Dr. Jeffrey Glanz, the Raine and Stanley Silverstein Chair in Professional Ethics and Values at Yeshiva University's Azrieli Graduate School of Jewish Education and Administration. As the author of 18 books and dozens of articles, Dr. Glanz knows his way around education. When you first meet Jeffrey, you see someone who you think is mild and reserved, and indeed he can be a bit quiet in a crowd. He looks like Jon Stewart with a beard, and has what I call "teacher's hands" that convey a gentle leadership as he waves them around during a lecture. But his is a backbone made of steel. His father survived the Holocaust, and along with courses in education that he teaches at Yeshiva, he also teaches classes on the Holocaust. This no doubt molded him as a child and would later inform his career in education at the deepest level with a compassion and sympathy for students that not many teachers possess.

Interestingly enough, Dr. Glanz was not the best of students himself when he was younger. He rebelled a bit and tried to just slide by for a while, which in turn has made him more sympathetic to those students who are straddling the fence so to speak. So many teachers are ready to write-off any student that is not sitting in the front row with their hands constantly in the air. Glanz knows better. You will not find a harder working professor anywhere, and yet he knows where he came from. I'd bet that there are legions of students in the New York area who remember Dr. Glanz as the turning point in their educational careers.

When I worked with him at Wagner College in New York, he was one of the students' favorite professors. I noticed that he was willing to lose a battle or two to win the war, and I have always admired that trait in leaders who can see the whole picture. He chose not to get mired in the little battles, but to keep his eye on the prize. I try to do the same myself.

Before Glanz was a professor, he taught in the New York City public schools for many years. Glanz recently came across a piece he had earlier written about a student he had while he was teaching forth grade in the South Bronx. Shaheim was a problem student, and it was only Glanz's second year of public school teaching, barely out of graduate school. All of us who have been public school teachers had students that made us happy when they *didn't* show up for school, unfortunately, Shaheim was usually present.

Glanz recalls that Shaheim loved school, even though his behavior was horrible, and that he would do anything and everything to aggravate Glanz.

> He appeared to love school, or shall I say loved to make my day a horror. He would do anything and everything to get under my skin. His senseless tapping of the pencil on his desk, despite my protestations, and his throwing papers around the room annoyed me to no end. Hardly a day passed without Shaheim getting into a physical fight, harassing a fellow student, or arguing with a teacher or fellow student. I was at my wits end. I tried everything I learned in college. Positive reinforcement didn't work, nor did time-out. Private consultations with him were short-lived and his parents were no help. In fact, they looked to me to "solve" his problems. Visits to the assistant principal's office provided momentary respites, but before too long Shaheim was back in class. I referred him to guidance and even suggested he be tested for learning disabilities or something. Reports came back that he was fine and "normal." Never once, by the way, did they observe his behavior while in class. To make a long story a bit shorter, Shaheim made it through fourth grade, but I barely did.

It makes me tired just reading this passage, because I too have been there as a middle school teacher.

Six years later, Glanz recalled a surprising visit. Someone wanted to meet with him during his lunch break; it was Shaheim. Glanz was shocked to see the tall, well-dressed young man standing before him. Shaheim told Glanz that "thanks to him," he was a successful high school student. Glanz couldn't believe his ears! But Shaheim went on to say that he was glad Glanz was "rough" with him, that other teachers had thrown him out of their classes, but that Glanz never gave up on him. He remembers the talks with Glanz during lunches at school, and said "you never gave up on me … you cared" Glanz was indeed stunned, but touched, and uses this story to this day to tell future teachers that we do make a difference after all, even when we don't think we do (J. Glanz, personal communication, April 20, 2009).

ALBERT CAMUS

Albert Camus was one of the greatest philosophers of all time. He was one of the main forces behind existentialism (though he would later deny that he was an existentialist) and won the Nobel Prize for Literature in 1957. *The Myth of Sisyphus*, written in 1942, tells the tale of Sisyphus, a Greek mythic figure, who is doomed to roll the same giant boulder up the mountain, only to have it roll down again. Camus was trying to convey how the human condition is absurd, and that the fulfillment in life lies not with the finish line, but with the journey.

Camus had a teacher that changed his life, an elementary school teacher named Louis Germain. The Camus-Germain relationship is arguably one of the most famous influences of a teacher on his pupil. Camus was the novelist, playwright, and philosopher who has been part of the Western canon for more than a half century. In 1957, after winning his Nobel Prize in Literature, he promptly wrote an eloquent thank you note to his former teacher who saved him from "want and ignorance" (Camus, 1995, p. 145).

Camus warmly portrays Germain in his unfinished autobiographical novel *The First Man*, published in 1995 long after Camus' death in 1960 from an automobile accident. We are told that Germain's class "was always interesting for the simple reason that he loved his work with a passion" (p. 143). Students in Germain's class "felt for the first time that they existed and that they were objects of the highest regard: they were judged worthy to discover the world" (p. 146). His method also "consisted of strict control on behavior while at the same time making his teaching lively and entertaining" (p. 144).

But what distinguished Germain more as a teacher was the role he played in his students' lives. These boys from Algeria came from families who were desperately poor and who had severely limited life choices. Camus' father had died in World War I and he was raised in a female-headed family where the grandmother was the dominant person. No parental figure could read or write. The grandmother's design for Camus was to help relieve the families' poverty by apprenticing the boy to a local tradesman. But Germain was successful in persuading the grandmother to have Camus try for a scholarship to the lycee which would continue to the baccalaureate. Along with three other similar boys, his best pupils, Germain tutored the boys at no charge 2 hours each night after school for a month to prepare them for the scholarship examination. Germain possessed that extra something that showed these students that he cared. It may or may not have been his brilliance with the content, but it just might have been the sheer willingness to be there for them.

Here is what Camus, fresh from his speech in Stockholm, had to say to his former teacher:

Dear Monsier Germain,

I let the commotion around me these days subside a bit before speaking to you from the bottom of my heart. I have just been given far too great an honor, one that I neither sought nor solicited. But when I first heard the news, my first thought, after my mother, was of you. Without you, without the affectionate hand you extended to the small poor child that I was, without your teaching, and your example, none of all this would have happened. I don't make too much of this sort of honor. But at least it gives me an opportunity to tell you what you have been and still are to me, and to assure you that your efforts, your work, and the generous heart you put into it still lives in one of your little schoolboys who, despite the years, has never stopped being your grateful pupil. I embrace you with all my heart.

Albert Camus (1995, p. 331)

W.E.B. DUBOIS

Another instance of an educator changing a student's life course involved the relationship of the civil rights leader, W.E.B. Dubois and his high school principal Frank Hosmer. DuBois, an African American, was living in the overwhelmingly White town of Great Barrington, MA, and had little expectation to rise above his situation. But DuBois recalls in his autobiography that it all changed:

The fact that I was going (to college) had been settled in my own mind from the time that my school principal, Frank Hosmer, had recommended my high school course. He suggested, quite as a matter of course, that I ought to take the college preparatory course.... If Hosmer had been another sort of man, with definite ideas to a Negro's "place" and had recommended agriculture or domestic economy, I would have doubtless have followed his advice ... I did not realize that Hosmer was quietly opening college doors for me. (Dubois, 1968, p. 101)

Moreover, Hosmer played a further crucial role in sending DuBois to college. An orphan "without a cent of property," with a grandfather "that was growing old, and had little," DuBois's dream of attending Harvard, his first choice because it "was the oldest, and largest and most widely known," seemed unrealistic (p. 102). But Hosmer enlisted two colleagues to help finance DuBois's college costs; a private school principal and a minister. DuBois recalled that "these three White men ... seemed to have clear ideas about my future." (p. 102).

Because of his youth and the fact that his high school "was below the standard of Harvard entrance requirements" he first attended the historically Black college Frisk in Tennessee in the segregated South (p. 102). After Frisk he enrolled at Harvard majoring in philosophy and becoming a protégé of the great American pragmatist philosopher William James. He recalled in his autobiography that he "was repeatedly a guest in the home of William James; he was my friend and guide to clear thinking" (p. 143). It was the era of Harvard's golden age of philosophy and DuBois commingled with world renowned philosophers Josiah Royce and George Santayana in addition to James. He was to graduate cum laude in philosophy and gave a commencement address that was widely praised in the press. It is ironic that one of the major advocates for a Black identity for African Americans, to be led by a talented tenth of Black leadership, should have his educational opportunity indebted to Whites (p. 143).

BRIAN GREENE

Dr. Brian Greene is a professor of mathematics and physics at Columbia University. He is one of only a handful of scientists in the world who has a mission to take physics to the general public. Dr. Greene's research focuses on superstring theory, which is a possible "theory of everything," currently the holy grail of physics. As it stands now, there is a disconnect between quantum physics and general relativity in that the laws that govern each don't match up. Albert Einstein sought to unite these two camps the whole of his adult life, but failed to uncover a unified theory that would explain both.

I first saw Dr. Greene during a lecture he was giving at the 92nd St. Y in New York City during the fall of 2000. We were *almost* the first people in line, of course, being that my husband the former New Yorker must always be overly punctual. I say that we were almost the first people in line, because in front of us, standing there alone, was a lovely woman who was looking through a catalogue. After a few minutes, she turned to us and smiled and after a few pleasantries asked; "what brings you to this lecture?" I mentioned that I taught science education at a university and that

Brian Greene was my favorite person in physics. So we in turn asked her what had brought her here? "I'm Brian's mother!" Quite a wonderful moment. During the long wait to enter the lecture hall, she showed me her catalogue and asked me to help her pick out a sofa. We also learned what time to show up at our favorite New York restaurant, the Four Seasons, and who to request as a waiter. Various cousins of the Greene's trickled in and so I was duly introduced to them as well. This made for an unforgettable day, and the lecture hadn't even begun yet.

At first look, Brian Greene is not what you would expect for a leading worldwide expert in physics. We are all use to the Einsteinein or Bill Gates ideal of the brilliant, somewhat incoherent and disheveled sockless scientist, so busy with hatching ideas that they can't find their keys. But Greene is different, and this difference no doubt is one of the reasons mobs of people flock to hear him speak. First, he looks as if he stepped off the cover of *GQ*; that is the first surprise. Then you hear him speak and the eloquence he has with the English language rivals that of endowed English professors and politicians named Kennedy. A unique combination of scientific and linguistic abilities, right and left brain firing in unison on all pistons. I've seen Dr. Greene several times, and even had the honor to have dinner with him as a guest at the home of the president of Old Dominion University. I talked so much the other guests kept looking at me like I had lost my mind. I was nervous and my science hero was eating string beans two feet away from me, so hopefully I can be forgiven. What I've learned from Greene over the years is that his ideas of teaching science are closely aligned with my own. I wondered if science isn't better taught conceptually first with the mathematics added later. I asked him this question during an e-mail exchange after that first lecture in New York.

> I think learning science conceptually is where the real fun is. It's the way to turn people on to the wonder of it all. But if students want to join the ranks of the researchers, they have ultimately to come to grips with the math. And for some this is painful. But I do think putting the math second is the way to go. All the best, Brian. PS My mother was duly flattered by this email! (B. Greene, personal correspondence, December 7, 2000)

I used this idea in my article "A Conceptual Model for Middle School Science Instruction" (Berube, 2000, p. 315), because I feel it is extremely important for teachers to grab students in science early on. Then and only then will they get the background to make decisions later about entering serious science fields, enabling them to conduct real research using mathematics to uncover the mysteries of physics. I believe that Dr. Greene does a huge service to this country (and the world) with his style of presenting and teaching science.

The most recent time I heard him speak was in June 2009, at the World Science Festival in New York City; the same festival in which I saw Neil de Grasse Tyson. Greene was giving the keynote lecture of the whole conference at the Skirball Center at New York University. The lecture was entitled, "Infinite Worlds: A Journey through Parallel Universes." The World Science Festival is the dreamchild of Dr. Greene and his wife Tracy Day, herself an Emmy award-winning journalist. Greene's passion for spreading the gospel of science infuses the whole event. The festival takes place in venues all over Manhattan and offers a diverse selection of events; from lectures by the world's most famous and important scientists, dance, music, performances, and a Greenwich Village street fair, all in the name of science for the masses. Of course, in the audiences of these events you will find serious scientists and colleagues of the speakers, along with professors, actors, movie stars, teachers, and regular people who happen to love science. I've heard a 10-year-old stand up and ask a Nobel Prize-winning physicist a question during a question and answer session following a lecture. And the speakers always receive standing ovations. It always reassures me to see science given this much love and respect, especially in the current anti-intellectual environment in which we find ourselves.

It is the theme we hear over and over again from leading scientists the world over. Capture the imagination, then the details of the mathematics will actually be easier to learn. Teach from the top-down. Concepts, ideas, imagination. Convert the young into lovers of science; then the shortage of American scientists will resolve itself.

FRANK MCCOURT

One of my favorite authors of all time was an Irish-American named Frank McCourt. McCourt won the Pulitzer Prize in Literature in 1997 and the National Books Critics Circle Award in 1996 for his memoir *Angela's Ashes*, a fantastic book of his poverty-stricken childhood in Limerick, Ireland. But perhaps his greatest crowning achievement was not the coveted Pulitzer, but his unbelievable success in the American classroom.

In 2005, he wrote a book called *Teacher Man* which is the best book I've ever read about the teaching profession, filled with truth, honesty, and hilarious accounts of McCourt's 30-year climb up the public school food chain in New York City. McCourt started his career at McKee Vocational and Technical High School on Staten Island, New York. On the first day he nearly gets fired for eating a sandwich, which a student has tossed to the floor. The sandwich was made by the boy's Italian mother and looked too good for McCourt to pass up, and anyway it got the attention of the students, who had been acting up. On the second day he nearly gets fired for joking that in Ireland, people go out with sheep after a student asks him if Irish people date (Wikipedia, n.d.-b).

McCourt also taught English as a second language, and took some African American students to a production of Hamlet. In a stroke of brilliance in order to get the students to write creatively, McCourt assigned them to write an excuse note from Adam to God. I cannot imagine a more creative and funny way to get students to write. He would also love to tell anecdotes about his childhood in Ireland, which would later become his memoirs, *Angela's Ashes* and *'Tis: A Memoir*. He spent most of the latter part of his teaching career at Stuyvesant High School in Manhattan, one of the best high schools in the United States, where he taught English and creative writing.

McCourt had a personality trait that resonates with me and that I find endearing, and that is his mistrust for authority and his distaste for rules. I have found in my own life and career that there are teachers who follow rules, and they usually keep their administrators very happy, and then there are those that care more about their students than they do about rules. Now rules are necessary, but they are there as a guide, and McCourt understood this. It was willingness to bend rules that won over so many students.

During the writing of this book, I had contacted several people who I felt had inspired their students, and Frank McCourt was the first person I contacted for an interview. Through his publicist at Simon and Schuster, who asked me for some available dates for a phone interview, I began to set something up. But throughout this time frame, Mr. McCourt was battling melanoma, which he had under control, but which finally overtook him in July, 2009. I was heartbroken. Not because of the missed interview, but because one of my biggest teacher role models and favorite authors was gone, along with any future books I would have savored over and over again.

Since I did not get the opportunity to speak with him, here's what his students have to say about him. These excerpts are taken from a *New York Times* blog dated from July 19, 2009, entitled *Share Your Memories of Frank McCourt*.

July 19, 2009 9:53 P.M.

He was a legend in the halls. I was never privileged enough to get a spot in one of his English classes, but I sat captivated by the stories of my classmates who did, and relished every moment.

—Nicole

July 19, 2009 10:01 P.M.

Frank McCourt, Pulitzer Prize winner died today after a long battle with Malignant Melanoma. My heart is broken. Frank was my teacher at Stuyvesant H.S. in English so long ago. He brought Melville alive in his classroom. He inspired me to write some amazing essays and always made his students feel special. I will mourn his loss along with millions of others. My heart remains broken. Faith Auslander Reilly class of 1975 Stuyvesant HS

—Faith Reilly

July 19, 2009 10:26 P.M.

He laughed and sneered, entertained and enthralled me and 30 other kids. We read "You Can't Go Home Again" and "My Papa's Waltz," wrote children's stories, sang songs and assigned ourselves our own grades (0-100). His writings truly capture the magic of his classroom. He was a good soul and will be missed.

—Diane '86

July 19, 2009 11:04 P.M.

I will always be honored to have been in Mr. McCourt's English class twice during my years at Stuyvesant. He was an inspiration to those students who cared. Yes, there were sandwich throwing types at Stuy. He would stop the class from time to time and read excerpts from his own childhood long ago in the 70's. I still remember the story of him picking up pieces of coal sitting on the curb, waiting for his father ...

Mr. McCourt was a great teacher. He wanted the students to tell their own stories and we often had readings of student's creative writing. One thing we shared was our immigrant experience. Having moved from Taiwan to the U.S. in the early 70's, life was different in terms of how we lived and how we tried to build a new life this new country. I remember for one class assignment, we were asked to write a book review. I chose Pearl Buck's The Good Earth which chronicled the life of a peasant family through famine and poverty and hope for better prospects. I compared the hardships of the characters of the book with my own parents who fled the Japanese then the Communists. Mr. McCourt gave encouraging comments on what families experience together. I have saved that one paper since then.

I was so proud when I learned that he wrote Angela's Ashes and won the Pulitzer Prize. Mr. McCourt deserved recognition. Not for the award or that he is a great story teller; but for his humanity. He showed me that the pains of life can also make you stronger and be a better person. In the darkest hours of his childhood, he was able to find those glimmers of hope and move forward.

—Hoantee

July 19, 2009 11:08 P.M.

I was privileged to have Frank McCourt as my creative writing teacher at Stuyvesant. Every day he taught us to think for ourselves, from our own experiences. He taught us the magic of language and the poetry of everyday existence. I was blessed to have his encouragement to start an underground newspaper when our school paper was censored, and will never forget going over galleys at the White Horse or Lion's Head. Rest in peace Mr. McCourt, you will be well missed and deeply remembered.

—Susan Manber Stuyvesant '81

July 19, 2009 11:10 P.M.

When I was one of many of Frank McCourt's students at Stuyvesant, he never struck me as anything more than a good teacher. His quiet style often overpowered his brilliant writing.

Looking back, I realize that it took him a while to be able to convey to the rest of us several lifetimes worth of anguish, sorrow and hope in his wonderful books and writings. He was a modest man never broken by his harsh beginnings and strong enough to persevere and become the great influence he was on many many students and fans alike.

May God bless you....

—Kathy B Huang

July 19, 2009 11:14 P.M.

In my senior year in Stuyvesant, I was privileged to take Mr. McCourt's class three times a day. Once, scheduled, in the morning, after lunch during a free period, and then again after that by cutting my economics class which I hated and wasn't going to learn anything at anyway.

I consider Mr. McCourt to be a huge influence on my life and my writing —and I am sometimes amazed at the number of journalists, poets, and writers of all stripes who got their start sitting in that classroom laughing at his stories.

— Arthur Jolly

Source: New York Times (2009).

There are 19 such pages, and of course I couldn't include everyone's comments here. I believe however that this is the true measure of a teacher—what may be said about you after you are gone. If this man, who survived a "miserable childhood," could face life with this much humor and compassion, then whom among us cannot? Frank McCourt was a special teacher, one who possessed that extra something that made a difference.

I have included many people in this chapter on favorite teachers that have personally made a huge impression on me; not as their student, but as an admirer of their work. A recurring theme that seems to appear is not necessarily the brilliance of these people (though they are certainly brilliant), but is more of an emotional attachment. Here are some of the many statements my subjects used to describe their favorite teachers:

- He made me feel important.
- She challenged me.
- Was funny.
- Was available to us.
- Knew their content.
- Conveyed "romance" for science.
- Demanded respect for each other.
- Had charisma.
- Stressed imagination.
- Was demanding and had high expectations.
- Exposed us to the best literature.
- Was caring.
- Was passionate about his subject.
- Loved his work with a passion.
- Had good control over behavior.
- Was there for us.
- Had a generous heart.
- Was affectionate.
- Was generous.
- Broke rules.
- Conquered adversity.

Anyone reading this list of traits would say that these teachers had the "X" factor indeed.

CHAPTER 6

THE BEAUTY OF SCIENCE TEACHING

What in the world does charisma have to do with science teaching, you may be asking? The importance of charisma in science teaching is subject of chapter 7, but it is related to the beauty of science. Neil deGrasse Tyson mentioned in a previous chapter that one does not need an abundance of charisma teaching at the graduate level. Graduate students of the sciences at the university level are not interested in charming professors, only generous ones who will help them with their research and to get published. Graduate level science students are the choir, we don't have to preach to them. They are already here, heart, body, and soul. Science is one of those rare subjects that require a special sort of person to teach it, lest either frustration or boredom set in and turn students off. We know that charming people, and people with personal charisma, seem to get life to go their way more often than those with less charming personalities. So why is it important for science teachers to have charisma? We have to win students over to science, charm them if you will, in order for them to experience the beauty of science they might not experience otherwise.

BACKGROUND

The reasons are many, and they begin with our current cultural climate against all things cerebral. The United States has a problem with intellec-

The "X" Factor: Personality Traits of Exceptional Science Teachers
pp. 59–76

tuals. No matter that America was founded by the foremost intellectuals of the day, we in the United States have become suspicious of anyone who claims to think for a living. During the last presidential campaign, American intellectuals were called "un-American," and "not *real* Americans." Other terms aimed at intellectuals in derogatory ways, are "cultural elite," and "socialists." Some have even begun to classify certain parts of the country as "real" versus "elite," with the elite being mostly Eastern coastal cities. (The word elite use to be a compliment, now it is considered a slam). The terms "egghead" and "nerd" are all but unheard of in Europe, where intellectuals proudly go about their business. But in America, we have become ashamed of our intellectual heritage. Why is this so?

Historian Richard Hofstadter spoke of this phenomenon in his famous 1963 book *Anti-Intellectualism in American Life*. M. Berube wrote in *Beyond Modernism and Postmodernism: Essays on the Politics of Culture* (2002), "The intellectual class," he (Hofstadter) wrote, "is of necessity an elite in manner of thinking and functioning." Any form of elitism, Hofstadter argued, cuts against the grain of "democratic institutions and the egalitarian sentiments of the country." In other words, Americans are more comfortable with ordinary Joes than braniac Einsteins" (p. 4).

Partially as a result of this rampant anti-intellectualism, America has fallen behind many other countries in math and science achievement. *The Washington Post* published a story on December 5, 2007, entitled "U.S. Teens Trail Peers Around World on Math-Science Test" (Glod, 2007). Here is what this study indicated:

> The disappointing performance of U.S. teenagers in math and science on an international exam, in scores released yesterday, has sparked calls for improvement in public schools to help the country keep pace in the global economy. The scores from the 2006 Program for International Student Assessment showed that U.S. 15-year-olds trailed their peers from many industrialized countries. The average science score of U.S. students lagged behind those in 16 in 30 countries in the Organization for Economic Cooperation and Development, a Paris-based group that represents the world's richest countries. The U.S. students were further behind in math, trailing counterparts in 23 countries. (para. 1-2)

The Virginian Pilot published an article (May 31, 2009) entitled, "U.S. Students Fare Poorly in Biosciences; Fast-Growing Industry Will be Short Qualified Workers, Report Finds." Stephanie Majors of the Associated Press states

> Middle and high school students across the country are generally falling behind in life sciences, and the nation is at risk of producing a dearth of qualified workers for the fast-growing bioscience industry, according to a

report. Students are showing less interest in taking life sciences and science courses, and high schools are doing a poor job of preparing students for college-level science, says the report, funded and researched by Columbus, Ohio-based Batelle, the Biotechnology Industry Organization and the Biotechnology Institute. The deficiencies will hurt the country's competitiveness with the rest of the world in the knowledge-based economy, the report concludes. (Major, 2009, p. 6)

The report also found that there are not enough well-qualified high school biology teachers, with one-in-eight biology teachers not certified to teach biology. These findings do not bode well for the future of the United States, since biosciences include the pharmaceutical, agriculture, and research in medical laboratories areas of science. The implications are frightening.

While anti-intellectualism offers one theory, Malcolm Gladwell offers another interesting explanation for why Americans lag behind other countries in math and science, especially Asian countries. In his book *Outliers: The Story of Success* (2008a), Gladwell includes a chapter he calls "Rice Paddies and Math Tests" (p. 224). This chapter seeks to explain why Asians seem to have the upper hand in math. It seems to be a combination of factors, including something Gladwell calls "rice paddy culture," which describes the excruciating work ethic held by Chinese who grow rice. Rice agriculture differs from American agriculture in ways that lay the foundation for this work ethic, which includes much, much longer hours in the rice field, "engineering" the rice paddy to exact specifications, an acceptance of a work ethic in their society so severe that they don't have summer vacations, which is in direct contrast to the American model of long summer vacations.

This holds true for schooling also. Asian children go to school longer than American children, both during the school day, and over the course of the school year. Asian students show a determination in solving problems that most Western students give up on after a few minutes. Gladwell attributes this to the rice paddy culture, where problems are worked on until solved, period.

Another huge advantage the Chinese have is in their language, which is more conducive toward math. In other words, it takes less time for Chinese children to count to 40, because their words for numbers are shorter. They also have a more sensible way of describing math principles, due to the way their language is set up. For example, if we try to add 27 plus 52 in our heads, most of us would have trouble, or have to grab a pencil and a piece of paper. But in China, where the number 27 is spoken as "two ten seven," and 52 is spoken as "five ten two," well then it becomes extremely simple to come up with the answer after only a moment's thought … the answer is 79. The Chinese language is *made* for math. "By the age of five, in other words, American children are already a *year* behind their Asian counterparts in the most fundamental of math skills" (p. 229).

But there is something else that contributes to this superiority in math, something so huge that it is probably the single most important advantage Asians have over Americans, and it is *attitude*. This attitude is conducive to intellectual pursuits, and unlike the American anti-intellectualism, fosters pride in academic accomplishment. According to Gladwell, Asians have a built-in attitude for success in math. Chinese rice farmers know that hard work will bring in a successful crop of rice. Russian farmers say that God is the one who decides if the crop is successful or not. So the Chinese place the locus of control for success with themselves. This attitude allows them to work on a problem *until it is solved*, and not before. Eggheads? They don't know the word. It has no importance to them. What is important is hard work and success. Asians are proud to be *exceptional*, while Americans are proud to be *average*. Indeed, Americans are *suspicious* of those of us that are not "average." This attitude infiltrates almost every layer of American life, even though those Americans guilty of it would deny it. This is a huge contributing factor as to why American children lag behind so many other countries in math and science.

Asia also does not have a problem with women scientists, and encourages them in all scientific fields. The American notion of male superiority in math and science is all pervasive in our culture. Girls are told that they are not really great at math from childhood. There is also a myth that girls and boys are "hardwired" for certain behaviors, and that little can be done to change this. Sharon Begley (2008) wrote a great article in *Newsweek* that addresses this issue, called "Math Is Hard, Barbie Said." Begley speaks to the notion that girl's brains are not "hardwired" for math. Begley uses information from two research findings to bolster her argument that there is no such thing as a hard-wired brain:

- First, that the left side of the brain controls the right side of the body and visa versa, but when stroke victims recover, their healthy portion of their brain takes over all functions.
- Second, when people are blindfolded for a week and receive intense tactile stimulation (reading Braille with their fingers), their visual cortex takes away valuable real estate in the brain devoted to the eyes, and lends it to the fingertips.

This evidence for the plasticity of the brain is also found in Norman Doidge's book *The Brain That Changes Itself* (2007). As Dr. Doidge mentions in his preface:

This book is about the revolutionary discovery that the human brain can change itself, as told through the stories of the scientists, doctors, and patients who have together brought about these astonishing transformations. Without operations or medications, they have made use of the brain's hitherto unknown ability to change. (p. xvii)

With decades and hundreds of years of the belief that our brains are hard-wired, little girls *believe* it when they are told that boys are good at math and science, and they aren't. And since we become what we believe we can become, it becomes a reality for so many little girls.

Pull culture back into this discussion, and our cultural beliefs about intellectuals, girls, math, and science, and you have a perfect recipe for American feminine underachievement or lack of achievement in these fields. As Begley (2008) states, "So what accounts for the small number of U.S. women earning doctorates in math (29%), holding tenure-track appointments in university math departments (19%), and winning the Fields Medal, the math "Nobel" (0%)? It's cultural. In countries that send a different message—that you can get good at science and math by hard work—females do better. In the International Mathematical Olympiad, a grueling 9-hour competition, the Bulgarian, German, and Russian teams have historically had strong female representation, while the U.S. team had no girls for 23 straight years (p. 57).

Begley also mentions a stunning study conducted by Maryjane Wraga of Smith College in 2007, which showed how social and cultural beliefs can de-rail feminine math and science performance. "Students were told that girls were less able at spatial intelligence just before they took a challenging test—and girls proceeded to do poorly on the part of the test that measured spatial ability. Brain scans revealed that as they took the test, girls had higher activity in their anterior cingulated (the site of negative emotions such as anger and sadness) and lower activity in the parts of the brain that handle visual and complex working memory. Anxiety triggered by social forces had muted activity required for spatial reasoning" (p. 57).

Brain studies reveal that thoughts produce certain brain chemicals, and these chemicals can either create pathways in the brain, or disengage them. Children become good at math by believing that they can do it (societal belief system), then by practicing for extended periods of time until these pathways are created, then reinforced by continuous use over the years. Doidge (2007) calls this a "mind map." Humans create mind maps in our brains, areas of the brain devoted to certain constructs. People who have been blind since birth have a mind map that is different from a seeing person, in that the seeing person has more area devoted to visual processing than the visually impaired person, but the blind person has a bigger mind map devoted to hearing and fingertip sensations for reading Braille.

Doidge (2007) also mentions how motivation creates larger mind maps. If girls believe early on that they can't do math or science, they are not motivated to *try*. Human motivation is an evolutionary phenomenon, and with limited time and resources, humans will only pursue goals that provide a return on their "effort investment." Doidge gives an example of an experiment with monkeys who were trained to touch a spinning disk with their fingertips with just the right amount of pressure for 10 seconds to get a food reward. After thousands of trials, the mind maps of these monkeys were measured and the area mapping the monkey's fingertips had grown. "The experiment showed that when an animal is motivated to learn, the brain responds plastically" (p. 66). So if girls are told as children that they cannot be successful in math or science, and they learn not to try, then this *belief* will physically alter their brains, thereby dedicating less brain "square footage" to the area that handles mathematics (what fires together wires together), and so begins a vicious cycle of mathematics and science underachievement in American females. (Remember, Asian girls have mind maps larger than American girls in the area of the brain dealing with math, since they have believed since childhood that they are capable at math, which means that they pursue math, and get better at it as they go along. This is also a cycle, but a good one). But this is a learned difference, not a genetically predetermined one.

BEAUTY AND MIRACLES

Roger Penrose, one of the most important and accomplished physicists alive today, is the author of the very ambitious book *The Road to Reality: A Complete Guide to the Laws of the Universe* (2004). Penrose lives in Oxford, where he is the Emeritus Rouse Ball Professor of Mathematics. In his book, Penrose offers a guide to the underlying principles governing the behavior of our universe through the use of mathematics. The word *charm* according to Webster's dictionary, implies a "compelling attractiveness," and a trait that "fascinates, allures and delights" (Webster's Online, n.d.). We also call this beauty. Penrose argues that the most beautiful and elegant thing in the universe is mathematics. According to Penrose, "many of the ideas perceived to have achieved a major advance in physical theory will also be viewed as compellingly beautiful" (2004, p. 1038). Science educators are missing an opportunity if we don't emphasize the beauty of science early on. Science is exquisitely beautiful.

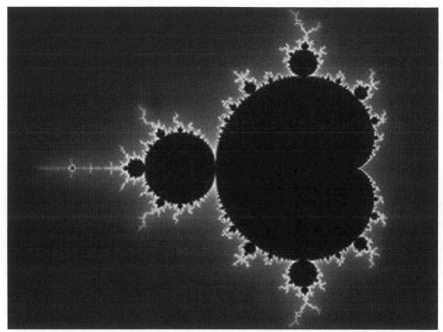

Source: Wikipedia (n.d.-c).

Figure 6.1. Example of the Mandlebrot set, a fractal created by mathematics. The edges of a Mandelbrot set has an elaborate boundry which does not simplify at greater magnification.

One of the most fascinating wonders of the world I have run across is fractals. According to Wikipedia, a fractal is "a rough or fragmented geometric shape that can be split into parts, each of which is (at least approximately) a reduced-size copy of the whole" (Wikipedia, n.d.-c). Fractals appear similar at all levels of magnification, are are considered infinitely complex. If you were able to loom above a fractal such as the Mandelbrot set, and suddenly become microscopic and zoom down into the set, there would be no end, and each deeper level would look exactly like the one you just left, on to infinity. Some beautiful examples of fractals are illustrated in Figures 6.1 to 6.11.

Figure 6.1 shows the Mandelbrot set—named after Benoit Mandelbrot, a French mathematician, and the "father" of fractal mathematics—

is a set of points in the complex plane, the boundary of which forms a fractal.… When computed and graphed on the complex plane the Mandelbrot Set is seen to have an elaborate boundary which does not simplify at any given magnification. (Wikipedia, n.d.-d)

Source: Wikipedia (n.d.-c).

Figure 6.2.   A second example of the Mandlebrot set, a fractal created by mathematics. The edges of this Mandelbrot set also have an elaborate boundry which does not simplify at greater magnification.

Source: Wikipedia (n.d.-d).

Figure 6.3.   Examples of fractals created by mathematics.

Source: MIQEL.com (n.d.).

Figure 6.4.   A head of Romanesco broccoli (a cross between broccoli and cauliflower).

Source: WebEcoist (n.d.).

Figure 6.5.   An example of a fractal found in nature illustrated by a shoreline.

Source: Original Beauty (n.d.).

Figure 6.6.   An example of a fractal found in nature: nautilus shell.

Source: Think Quest (n.d.).

Figure 6.7.   An example of a fractal found in nature: lightening

Mandelbrot argued that the artificially straight lines in Euclidian geometry were not a true representation of the real natural world like fractals are. The Mandelbrot set is created by humans by employing mathematics, but fractals occur in nature all the time. In nature, there are no straight lines. Every time you look at a mountain range, a head of broccoli, or a picture of the blood vessels in a lung, you are looking at natural fractals.

Fractals are also present in art (important for interdisciplinary instruction). Consider Figure 6.8. This picture was generated by a computer. But it is very much like the work of M.C. Escher, a Dutch artist who gave the world mind-blowing interpretations of reality in his art. Figures 6.9-6.11 are drawings by Escher that dramatically illustrate fractals.

Science teachers should be using concepts such as fractals to capture the imagination of science and math students in every grade level. Many careers also use fractal mathematics, including many of the special effects engineers who create scenery in movies we all watch. Employing fractals would also be an excellent way to teach across the curriculum. There is much mathematics in art, and making students aware of this would not only heighten their appreciation of art, but of science and math as well. Fractals are relevant to our everyday lives.

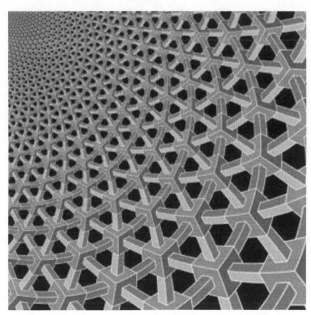

Source: ScienceDaily (n.d.).

Figure 6.8.   Man-made fractal illustrated by art.

Source: Temel Nosce (n.d.).

Figure 6.9.   "Heaven and Hell" by M. C. Escher (1960). Escher created several works that depended on the interwoven relationship between two different figures, in this case bats and angels.

Brian Greene had beauty in mind when he wrote his 1999 book, *The Elegant Universe: Superstrings, Hidden Dimensions, and the Quest for the Ultimate Theory.*" He describes supersymmetry this way:

"Physicists describe these two properties of physical laws—that they do not depend on when or where you use them—as *symmetries* of nature. By this usage physicists mean that nature treats every moment in time and every location in space identically symmetrically—by ensuring that the same fundamental laws are in operation. Much the same manner that they affect art

Source: The Domain for Truth (n.d.).

Figure 6.10.   "Ascending and Descending" by M. CEscher, 1960. In this work, Escher illustrates a staircase that seems to go nowhere.

and music, such symmetries are deeply satisfying; they highlight an order and a coherence in the workings of nature. The elegance of rich, complex, and diverse phenomena emerging from a simple set of universal laws is at least part of what physicists mean when they invoke the term 'beautiful'" (p. 169).

Source: Artist Market (n.d.).

Figure 6.11.   Wood engraving and woodcut in black and brown, by M. C. Escher (1956). This engraving illustrates the endless interplay between lizards.

Greene also makes the connection between superstring theory and music. Instead of the old fashioned idea of an atom, "strings" may be vibrating particles similar to violin strings.

> Here's the central fact: Just as the different vibrational patterns of a violin string give rise to different musical notes, *the different vibrational patterns of a fundamental string give rise to different masses and force changes....* According to string theory, the properties of an elementary "particle"—it's mass and its various force charges-are determined by the precise resonant pattern of vibration that its internal string executes. (p. 144)

Science is a blend of logic and imagination, according to *Science For All Americans: Project 2061* (1991). In 1991, the American Association for the Advancement of Science commissioned this book as a reflection of their long-term initiative called "Project 2061." This initiative was and is to reform K-12 education in science, mathematics, and technology. Imagination remains a vital part of science, yet it is often neglected in favor of more quantitative and measurable science. Yet, it is these very ideas that give birth to experiments that can then in turn be quantified and measured. Science is always trying to make the complicated elegant, as in the equivalence principle. The equivalence principle is so named in order to demonstrate the indistinguishability between accelerated motion and gravity (Greene, 1999, p. 144). Even with $E = MC^2$, arguably one of the most difficult formulae of physics, has an elegant description. Albert Einstein, in a flash of imagination, "saw" his theory of relativity while daydreaming one day while at work as a patent clerk in Switzerland. He imagined himself riding a beam of light. The mathematics and years of study came afterward. Human imagination is so important, and so disrespected in modern education.

Leonard Shlain, a surgeon by trade, in his book *Art & Physics: Space, Time & Light* (1991), writes of the interconnection of beauty and science, using art as the foundation for his discussion. Shlain states

> artists and physicists share the desire to investigate the ways the interlocking pieces of reality fit together. This is the common ground upon which they meet ... the physicist, like any scientist, sets out to break "nature" down into its component parts to analyze the relationship of those parts. The process is principally one of reduction. The artist, on the other hand, often juxtaposes different features of reality and synthesizes them, so that upon completion, the whole work is greater than the sum of its parts. There is considerable crossover in the techniques used by both. The novelist Vladimir Nabokov wrote, "There is no science without fancy and no art without facts." (p. 16)

One can make the argument that the art of cubism and the science of physics are two sides of the same coin. When we look at the concept of wave-particle duality, we see that light has, *at the same time*, features of both waves and of individual particles. We also see the superposition principle, where a single particle such as an electron, can be in two places, also *at the same time*. How can this be, we ask? Such are the strange rules of quantum mechanics. Yet the art form known as cubism, made famous by artists such as Pablo Picasso, have introduced masterpieces such as his 1907 "Les Demoiselles d'Avignon," which set the art world on it's ear by depicting the front, sides, and back of women's' heads and bodies simultaneously. Is it any coincidence that the painting depicted in Figure 6.12 came out dur-

Source: Princeton University Blog Service (n.d.).

Figure 6.12.   Picasso's 1907 "Les Demoiselles d'Avignon."

ing the time Einstein was writing his theory of relativity? One can imagine the connection.

TEACHING SCIENCE TO EVERYONE

Teaching science at times can be a very frustrating endeavor. Science teachers run into students at all levels who don't "believe" in science. These students have certain religious or cultural beliefs, learned from childhood, that provide a lens through which they view the world. Creationists are people who take biblical teaching about the beginnings of the world literally, and who disavow all aspects of scientific proof of the age of the earth or fossils. It can be hugely frustrating trying to teach evolution or geology to students who believe the world is only 6,000 years old. A good science teacher, armed with knowledge of carbon dating (among other things) can strike the balance between teaching true science and keeping students interested who otherwise might be offended.

When professors of education prepare preservice science teachers for the classroom, science must be the first priority, however we also have to take into consideration the belief systems of those preservice teachers. Akerson and Donnelly (2008) offer this insight:

> Preservice teachers come to the science methods classroom holding many cultural values. We are not advocating that science educators change these values but that they recognize their existence and develop strategies that ameliorate tensions that may exist for some students in attaining adequate NOS (Nature of Science) views for some elements. For instance, science educators need to recognize that many preservice teachers strongly value security, spirituality, and tradition. As such, we need to find teaching approaches for improving views of tentative, creative, and subjective NOS without threatening these ways of knowing that our preservice 56 *Journal of Elementary Science Education* teachers believe are not subject to change. (pp. 55, 56).

But in reality, is this approach possible? Can a science teacher teach the facts about science without contradicting a student's beliefs? It is not in the best interest of science or the student to water down the curriculum in order to spare insult, but there is a way good teachers can teach specific science content while also respecting student belief systems. Here is a letter to the editor I wrote in *The Chronicle of Higher Education* as a rebuttal to an earlier article concerning this very topic ("Learning About God From Fossils," Berube, 2009):

> I have to respectfully disagree with Arri Eisen and David Westmoreland ("Teaching Science, With Faith in Mind," *The Chronicle,* May 1). A science professor's responsibility is to teach science in an objective way, which is the whole intent of the scientific method and is what separates science from other fields. We don't do our students any favors by watering down science.
>
> This dichotomy is artificial in the first place, because one can believe in God and in science—in fact, some of the best scientists who ever lived did just that (Einstein being just one). Nevertheless, I've run across problems when I was teaching the big bang or evolution and some of my students disagreed with me because they were raised with different beliefs and were taught different things. Where believers run into problems is in the "what happened when" time line. But science has math on its side, and we can pretty much say with surety how old a fossil is, for instance, because of technology like carbon dating. Who can argue with carbon dating?

Instead of arguing that something happened at a certain time, why not just open up to the possibility that God might have created the world just this way, with evolution and big bangs and millions of years of fossils? I've never had a problem with looking at evolution and considering how clever whoever did this must be. In fact, I believe that science will tell us more about God than any book. Science is thankfully not open to personal opinion, which makes it pure, like mathematics. To pull punches in the teaching of science does not move us forward. (p. A32).

It is imperative that we capture our children's imagination for science early on, while they still have a thirst for learning. This is why charm and charisma are so important and will be the subject of the next chapter.

CHAPTER 7

CHARISMA AND SCIENCE TEACHING CASE STUDIES

Is there a correlation between successful teaching and personality traits, such as charm and charisma? Do charismatic people hold greater power in influencing people to see things their way? Are charming people greater motivators? In the introduction I brought forth these traits, knowing full well that charm and charisma are not easy to measure, and have not historically been important measures when discussing teacher quality. But Dr. Howard Friedman of the University of California Riverside, has developed an instrument that he calls the "Affective Communication Test" (ACT). Dr. Friedman does research on such things as "self-healing personalities" and is interested in how personality affects health or illness. Malcolm Gladwell used this instrument in "The Tipping Point" to find a connection between charm and success (in general), and so I wanted to apply this to teacher personality traits to see if there was a correlation between charm and teacher success, but first a word about Gladwell's research.

In *The Tipping Point: How Little Things Can Make a Big Difference* (2000), Gladwell studies social epidemics that can be described on the back cover blurb as magical moments when an idea, trend, or social behavior crosses a threshold, tips, and spreads like wildfire. Gladwell explores the tipping point phenomenon, and the role we as humans play. He starts chapter 2 (The Law of the Few, p. 30) with a description of Paul Revere's famous

The "X" Factor: Personality Traits of Exceptional Science Teachers
pp. 77–81
Copyright © 2010 by Information Age Publishing

ride through Boston in 1775, and speaks of how certain people can play roles of connectors, mavens, and salesmen, in situations where information is passed along in society (social epidemics). (Doesn't teaching consist of passing along information in social situations?) Gladwell describes connectors as "people with a special gift for bringing the world together" (p. 38). Connectors always know lots of people, just like Paul Revere did. Mavens are those people who have accumulated so much knowledge that they know something about almost everything. Mavens have also heard things that they pass along; their desire is to educate and to help; they are teachers in a way. Yet, with all of their skills, they are not persuasive, which is where the salesmen come into play. The persuasive personality type is the last person in the chain needed to pull off a social phenomenon. Salesmen (these can be women too) are charming ... charismatic ... persuasive ... exuberant. These people can make you feel good from the outside-in; meaning that you "catch" their good moods from them.

Gladwell employed Friedman, Prince, Riggio, and DiMatteo's Affective Communication Test (1980), that measures "this ability to send emotion, to be contagious," in order to "test" the personalities of the subjects of his book to see if there would be a correlation between their success, and their ability to effectively (and *affectively*) communicate.

> The test is a self-administered survey, with thirteen questions relating to things like whether you can keep still when you hear good dance music, how loud your laugh is, whether you touch friends when you talk to them, how good you are at sending seductive glances, whether you like to be the center of attention. The highest possible score on the test is 117 points, with the average score, according to Friedman, somewhere around 71. (pp. 85, 86).

When Gladwell used the ACT to measure success, he was discussing a man named Tom Gau, in his chapter "The Law of the Few," which highlighted how some seem to sway people to their way of thinking, while others can't seem to, and the art of persuasion. (Isn't that what teaching is all about?) Gladwell describes Gau as a persuasive personality type, which comes in handy in his line of work as a financial planner. Gau makes millions of dollars a year persuading people to buy his product. Gau was referred to Gladwell by a behavioral psychologist, and was described as "mesmerizing." Gau loves his job and doesn't have to work anymore, but loves helping people. Gladwell asked Gau to take Friedman et al.'s charisma test, and out of a possible 117 points, scored a 116, extremely charismatic, and also persuasive.

To see what it means to be a high scorer, Friedman et al. conducted a study, the gist of which is that only charismatic people can infect other people in a room with his or her emotions, inexpressive people (low scorers) will "catch" the mood of the expressive person (high scorers), no matter what the expressive person's mood is (p. 85). He picked a few dozen people who had scored very high on his test—above 90—and a few dozen who scored very low—below 60—and asked them to fill out a questionnaire measuring how they felt "at this instant." He then put all of the high-scorers in separate rooms, and paired each of them with two low-scorers. They were told to sit in the room together for 2 minutes. They could look at each other, but not talk. Then, once the session was over, they were asked again to fill out a detailed questionnaire on how they were feeling. Friedman et al. found that in just 2 minutes, without a word being spoken, the low-scorers ended up picking up the moods of the high-scorers. If the charismatic person started out depressed, and the inexpressive person started out happy, by the end of the 2 minutes the inexpressive person was depressed as well. But it didn't work the other way. Only the charismatic person could infect the other people in the room with his or her emotions (p. 86).

This has huge implications in the classroom for the teaching profession, and so I became interested in a possible correlation between successful teaching and scores on the ACT.

My subjects were past and current teachers at all levels (grade school through college) who have gained recognition for outstanding teaching, either through awards or some other accolade for teaching from their school or university. My first subject was myself, since I received a teaching award during my years teaching middle school science. I had my other subjects take the ACT and scored them on it, and the results were enlightening. Some of these subjects are fairly quiet people, so personality types are not necessarily being measured in this instrument, only the ability to transmit and communicate emotion (charm, charisma, persuasion). As mentioned, the highest possible score on the ACT is 117, which would indicate very high charisma (or ability to communicate emotions). The average score is 71. Very high is indicated as above 90, very low is indicated as below 60. Table 7.1. presents the findings.

Here were the subjects that I tested:

- Clair Berube (myself), assistant professor of science education, former middle school science teacher and recipient of middle school teaching award. Score: 115.
- Gertrude Henry, associate professor of education, Hampton University, recipient of university teaching award. Score: 101
- Jeffrey Glanz, endowed professor of education, Yeshiva University, recipient of University teaching award. Score: 90
- Jill Dustin, associate professor of counseling and human services, Old Dominion University, recipient of numerous university teaching awards. Score: 101

**Table 7.1.   Normal Distribution of Affective
Communication Test Scores for the General Population**

Highest possible score = 117
Average = 71
Very High = over 90
Very Low = below 60
Percentile Rankings: Conversion of ACT scores to percentiles:

Score	Percentile of Population Scoring Lower Than This
39	2%
47	7%
55	16%
63	31%
71	50%
79	69%
87	84%
95	93%
103	98%

Note: ACT = Affective Communication Test. Scores represent Dr. Friedman's results from testing the general population.

- Garrett McAuliffe, university professor of counseling, Old Dominion University, recipient of numerous University teaching awards. Score: 94

- Thomas R. Smigiel, Jr., assistant principal, Granby High School, Norfolk, Virginia: 2008 Virginia Teacher of the Year, 2008 National Teacher of the Year Finalist. Score: 102

- Ed Neukrug, professor of counseling, Old Dominion University, recipient of University teaching award. Score: 88

- Sue McKinney, assistant professor of mathematics education, Old Dominion University, recipient of University teaching award. Score: 101

- Alexander Leidholdt, Ruth D. Bridgeforth Professor of Telecommunications, James Madison University, recipient of university teaching award. Score: 91

- Alan "Woody" Schwitzer, psychologist and professor, Department of Counseling and Human Services, Old Dominion University. Score: 100.

The average for this group is 98.3, which is 27 points higher than the average for the general population, and 8 points over the designation "very high." This group as an average scored better than 93% of all others who have ever taken this instrument, and underscores the notion that extra extraordinary teachers have personality traits which, though hard to measure, are present nonetheless and which contribute to outstanding teaching careers.

CHAPTER 8

TRANSLATING THESE TRAITS TO THE CLASSROOM

In chapter 1 we examined certain teacher dispositions and personality traits and what the current literature has to say about them. How do these traits play out in actual classrooms?

On December 15, 2008, Malcolm Gladwell wrote in his blog (Gladwell.com) an entry entitled "Most Likely to Succeed: How Do We Hire When We Can't Tell Who's Right for The Job?", which had been previously published by the *New Yorker*. In it, Gladwell uses first- and second-round draft pick football quarterbacks to discuss success on the job. Gladwell compares their preprofessional-career achievement, success, and high expectations, with the reality years later of what they actually achieved after being drafted into top teams. These players had the most unbelievable amount of potential, they were the highest achievers on their college teams, *they* were the ones that were supposed to become football superstars. These players dropped into obscurity. Why didn't their college success translate to major league success? The traits that appeared to obviously predict major leagues success didn't translate.

Gladwell then turns the topic of conversation to American classrooms, and the subject of teacher quality. He states; "After years of worrying about issues like school funding levels, class size, and curriculum design, many reformers have come to the conclusion that nothing matters more than finding people with the potential to be great teachers. But there's a

The "X" Factor: Personality Traits of Exceptional Science Teachers
pp. 83–89

hitch: no one knows what a person with the potential to be a great teacher looks like. The school system has a quarterback problem" (2008b). Gladwell goes on to include data from studies that suggest that the best teachers don't necessarily come from the best schools (many do), but that they have certain personality traits that ensure their success, and that these traits aren't measured effectively as predictors of success during teacher education.

Other research also shows a connection between certain personality traits and predictive teacher success. Thornton, Peltier, and Hill (2005) highlight the fact that there are not enough appropriate screening procedures in place to weed out who will and who will not be successful teachers. They also state that personality traits correlate with teaching success and length of service. Here are their research questions:

- What are the personality profiles of people who elect to become teachers?
- Are the personality profiles of potential teachers different from the profiles of other undergraduate students?
- Can personality profiles of preservice teachers be used to determine future success and longevity of classroom teachers?

Thornton et al. investigated the personality profiles of 175 college students, 72% of which had stated that they were going to seek teaching positions upon graduation. The researchers employed the Myers-Briggs Type Indicator (based on the work by Carl Jung). This instrument measures people on 16 personality types, thereby placing them into four dichotomous categories (see Table 1.1). The four dichotomies are: extroversion versus introversion, sensing versus intuition, thinking versus feeling, and judging versus perceiving. Table 8.1 illustrates the interaction of the four personality preferences.

Jung (1923) identified two pairs of psychological functions:

- The two *perceiving* functions, sensing and intuition
- The two *judging* functions, thinking and feeling

According to the Myers-Briggs typology model, each person uses one of these four functions more dominantly and proficiently than the other three; however, all four functions are used at different times depending on the circumstances.

Sensing and *intuition* are the information-gathering (perceiving) functions. They describe how new information is understood and interpreted. Individuals who prefer sensing are more likely to trust information that is

**Table 8.1.   The 16 Possible Personality Types
With the Corresponding Percentage of the American Population**

ISTJ	ISFJ	INFJ	INTJ
11.6%	13.8%	1.5%	2.1%
ISTP	ISFP	INFP	INTP
5.4%	8.8%	4.3%	3.3%
ESTP	ESFP	ENFP	ENTP
4.3%	8.5%	8.1%	3.2%
ESTJ	ESFJ	ENFJ	ENTJ
8.7%	12.3%	2.4%	1.8%

Note: Estimated percentages of the 16 types in the American population using inferential statistics (Wikipedia, n.d.-a). Descriptions of the dichotomies and types, according to Wikipedia (n.d.-a): Functions: Sensing (S) / iNtuition (N) and Thinking (T) / Feeling (F).

in the present, tangible and concrete: that is, information that can be understood by the five senses. They tend to distrust hunches that seem to come out of nowhere. They prefer to look for details and facts. For them, the meaning is in the data. On the other hand, those who prefer intuition tend to trust information that is more abstract or theoretical, that can be associated with other information (either remembered or discovered by seeking a wider context or pattern). They may be more interested in future possibilities. They tend to trust those flashes of insight that seem to bubble up from the unconscious mind. The meaning is in how the data relates to the pattern or theory.

Thinking and *feeling* are the decision-making (judging) functions. The thinking and feeling functions are both used to make rational decisions, based on the data received from their information-gathering functions (sensing or intuition). Those who prefer *thinking* tend to decide things from a more detached standpoint, measuring the decision by what seems reasonable, logical, causal, consistent and matching a given set of rules. Those who prefer feeling tend to come to decisions by associating or empathizing with the situation, looking at it "from the inside" and weighing the situation to achieve, on balance, the greatest harmony, consensus and fit, considering the needs of the people involved. As noted already, people who prefer thinking do not necessarily, in the everyday sense, "think better" than their feeling counterparts; the opposite preference is considered an equally rational way of coming to decisions (and, in any case, the MBTI assessment is a measure of preference, not ability). Similarly, those who prefer feeling do not necessarily have "better" emotional reactions than their thinking counterparts (Wikipedia, n.d.-a).

Thornton discovered that of the students who planned to seek teaching jobs (72%), the predominate personality type for them was the ESFJ (extrovert-sensing-feeling-judging). However, other research finds that most teachers are ENFJ (extroversion, intuition, feeling, judging) (Keirsey & Bates, 1984). Keirsey and Bates said that ENFJs have the following general characteristics:

- People are highest importance and priority (people more important than rules).
- Loyalty, commitment, and responsibility are important values.
- ENFJs prefer a work setting that focuses on changing things for the betterment of others. Interestingly, Keirsey reports that ENFJs represent only 7.5% of the general population; in our (Thornton) study group of preservice teachers only 10% were ENFJs (Thornton, p. 493).

As mentioned in chapter 1, Daugherty, Logan, and Turner (2003) also conducted a study that linked preservice teachers' psychological traits to their classroom performance ratings. After mentioning that personal qualities have an effect on work performance, they identify three traits: personality style, creative thinking, and motivation. I cite this study again here to remind the reader that good grades alone do not predict teacher success. Daughtery found that creative, people-centered teachers had more success and less burnout, and again, these traits are not easily measured.

Earlier in this book I stated that it is a shame that more creative people do not become teachers. In chapter 1, I suggest that the teaching profession needs more dreamers and rebels; people not so married to rules and regulations. There is research to support the notion that traits like nonconformity and creativity do indeed make for better teachers, especially in science. Meador (2003) writes:

> creative scientists differ from non-creative scientists in at least two distinct ways. First, creative scientists need to be *free of rules* (emphasis added) in order to exercise flexible thinking. This flexibility makes them more likely than others to know when to abandon nonproductive efforts and change approaches to problem solving. Second, creative scientists also seem to be more open to experience, making them more sensitive to problems than their non-creative colleagues...the creative scientist may also recognize a problem that others miss, and thus, possess great potential for producing original research (pp. 25-26).

Albert Einstein was famous for his rebellious streak, both as a student and as a scientist. He was well known for avoiding rules and conventions, both socially and academically. It was his rebelliousness that contributed to his free thinking style, which in turn provided fertile ground for his theories of relativity which literally changed the way we view the world. The leading scientists in the world ridiculed and demeaned him and thought him foolish for developing such a theory. Greatness always breaks away from the pack.

Einstein, one of the most creative scientists of all time, would tell people that he thought in pictures. In Walter Isaacson's biography, *Einstein: His Life and Universe* (2007), he includes a quote from Einstein: " 'I very rarely think in words at all,' he later told a psychologist. 'A thought comes, and I may try to express it in words afterwords' " (p. 9). Isaacson also includes many references to Einstein's famous rebellious streak. "A society's competitive advantage will come not from how well its schools teach the multiplication and periodic tables, but from how well they stimulate imagination and creativity" (pp. 6, 7). Therein lies the key, I think, to Einstein's brilliance and the lessons of his life. As a young student he never did well with rote learning. And later, as a theorist, his success came not from the brute strength of his mental processing power but from his imagination and creativity. As he once is said to have declared, "Imagination is more important than knowledge.' That approach required him to embrace nonconformity. 'Long live impudence!' ... 'it is my guardian angel in this world.'"(p. 7).

The combination of creativity and independent thinking was the magical formula for one of the greatest scientific discoveries of all humanity. "This outlook made Einstein a rebel with a reverence for the harmony of nature" (Isaacson, 2007, p. 7). His rebellious nature carried over into all areas of his life as well.

> Einstein's nonconformist streak was evident in his personality and politics as well. Although he subscribed to socialist ideals, he was too much of an individualist to be comfortable with excessive state control or centralized authority. His impudent instincts, which served him so well as a young scientist, made him allergic to nationalism, militarism, and anything that smacked of a herd mentality. (p. 4)

Luckily for us, this contempt for authority led him to question Newtonian physics, thereby upsetting hundreds of years of scientific status quo, and moving humanity closer to cosmic truth. These traits, which include independent thinking, creativity, rebelliousness, and lack of reverence for authority, made for the perfect scientist. Success in science cannot spring from a person who thinks convergently and who obeys all of the rules.

Do these traits ensure a successful science classroom? What exactly does the science classroom of an exceptional science teacher look like? How do these star teachers teach differently than the merely average? Ediger (2002) discovered that science teachers who possessed the more positive "attitudes" (dispositions) had statistically significant improvement in student achievement. The following were also found to be statistically significant:

- Teaching competency was related to attitudes toward teaching science.
- Teacher personality was related to attitudes in teaching science.
- Students of more competent teachers achieved significantly higher than those students who had less competent science teachers (p. 25).

Ediger goes on to say that 12 personality traits also must be present in science teachers (as quoted from a study by Cattell [1931]). These include (from most important): personality, will power, intelligence, sympathy, tact, open mindedness, enthusiasm, knowledge of psychology, pedagogy, technique, perseverance, industriousness (p. 27). Notice that personality and will power (strength of will) rank higher than intelligence.

A good teacher will also incorporate the natural rebel quality of most students mentioned earlier into his or her science class. The trait of rebelliousness is usually associated with students who are discipline problems, wayward teenagers, and school dropouts. This trait, unfortunately, has been overlook in most serious academic scholarship in terms of *positive* outcomes in education, and especially science education. I can think of no better content area for a teacher to "take advantage" of a student's rebelliousness and to channel it into a great outcome. Science by its very nature is divergent.

According to *Science For All Americans: Project 2061* (American Association for the Advancement of Science):

Science is a blend of logic and *imagination* [emphasis added] … scientific concepts do not emerge automatically from data or from any amount of analysis alone. Inventing hypotheses or theories to imagine how the world works and then figuring out how they can be put to the test of reality is as creative as writing poetry, composing music, or designing skyscrapers. (p. 5)

Also:

Science is not authoritarian: It is appropriate in science, as elsewhere, to turn to knowledgeable sources of information and opinion, usually people who specialize in relevant disciplines. But esteemed authorities have been wrong many times in the history of science … in the short run, new ideas that do not mesh well with mainstream ideas may encounter vigorous criticism, and scientists investigating such ideas may have difficulty obtaining support for their research. (p. 7)

So it appears that in order to be a successful scientist, a good rebellious streak is *required* for success!

In an article entitled "An Argument for Arguments in Science Class," Osborne (2009/2010) suggests that science is taught exactly opposite to its true nature, which is open inquiry and invention. Osborne also claims that critical thinking is needed for successful science learning, which is not very popular in a standards-driven society, only interested in convergent bubble test outcomes. The answer to this problem? "Giving students opportunities to construct arguments and counter arguments can be an effective strategy for both developing students' ability to reason *and* enhancing their conceptual understanding" (pp. 62, 63). In order for students to learn the art of proper argument technique, the teacher has to foster critical thinking (criticism) in ways that current theories are questioned and alternative ones are posed. Research points to success in this new way of teaching (Driver, Newton, & Osborne, 2000).

Not only would lively classroom debate and argument foster higher order learning skills, but they would also ensure higher student engagement and less discipline problems. According to Osborne (2009/2010),

> As Au (2007) has shown, NCLB (No Child Left Behind) has led to a greater emphasis on teaching to the test, a dominance of teacher-led pedagogy, and greater fragmentation—all features that diminish student engagement. Giving students opportunities to discuss, reason, and deliberate in science seems to offer one way to reverse that trend. If learning to argue is learning to think, then developing this facility in students may be the most enduring value of a good education. (p. 65)

CHAPTER 9

CONCLUSION

In chapter 5, I spoke of Brian Greene and Neil de Grasse Tyson and their inspirational love of science. I truly believe that they have the secret ingredient when it comes to teaching, and for science teaching in particular. A combination of content expertise, communication skills, and personality traits that combine for a superior experience for anyone who is lucky enough to be their student. Upon arriving home from my New York adventure at the science festival, I was inspired to write the following.

My husband and I emerge from the subway into the misty late afternoon air and stroll down Central Park West toward the Hayden Planetarium. We are walking in that confident way that New Yorkers do; after all, we lived there for a time, and if you live in New York for any amount of time, you are a New Yorker! It is June 2009 and the World Science Festival is in session, drawing dozens of the world's leading scientists and stars together for several days with the goal of bringing science to everyday people. There are talks, seminars, plays, performances, round tables, interviews and music.

We have tickets to three of the sessions, including one called "Time Since Einstein" at the John Jay College, CUNY in the upper west side. In this session, we listen to world famous scientists ask the question, "What is time?" The panel includes Sir Roger Penrose from the University of Oxford, philosopher David Albert from Columbia University, who convinces me that physics and philosophy are a perfect match, Sean Carroll from Caltech, and others. It is ironic that the session is about time,

The "X" Factor: Personality Traits of Exceptional Science Teachers
pp. 91–93
Copyright © 2010 by Information Age Publishing
All rights of reproduction in any form reserved.

because it seems that only 5 minutes elapse before it is over and the panel is receiving a standing ovation. We are also scheduled to see "Infinite Worlds; A Journey Through Parallel Universes," which is the keynote address of the festival. Brian Greene, professor of mathematics and physics at Columbia is the "star" of this talk, and with him are cosmologists Alan Guth, professor of physics at MIT, Andrei Linde from Stanford, and Nick Bostrom from Oxford University. Dr. Greene is famous for having that "X" factor, because he can discuss unbelievably difficult subject matter in a way that makes average people believe that they can learn anything. We leave the theater energized and awed by the vast knowledge of the panel, by their enthusiasm and humor, and with the way they can easily "infect" us with love for their topic.

But on this night, our first night in town, we are scheduled to attend a session entitled "Navigating the Cosmos" to be held at the Hayden Planetarium. The scientists scheduled to speak are Neil deGrasse Tyson, the director and subject of my interview earlier in the book, renowned physicists from the field of theoretical and astrophysics that include Jim Gates, University of Maryland, College Park and a member of President Obama's Council of advisors of science and technology, Lawrence Krauss from Arizona State University, and Evalyn Gates, the assistant director of the Kavli Institute for Cosmological Physics at the University of Chicago and a senior research associate in the Department of Astronomy and Astrophysics. We take our seats in the dark planetarium awaiting their arrival. Out walk the scientists, to a rock star ovation. Especially Tyson,who has a large following among lay people and scientists alike. He is signing autographs and getting his picture taken with fans, some of which are his students, as he inches closer to the center of the floor.

The lights are lowered in the planetarium. We sit back and look up at the stars. We are taken on a tour of the cosmos from the comfort of our seats, guided by the gifted scientists before us. During the talk, I notice the interplay of the scientists, the strengths of each, and the role each is playing in this discussion. I notice how Tyson is "translating" what the other scientists are saying, and each time he does it, the audience makes an almost audible "ohhh" sound, as if to say "oh, ok … we get it now" Tyson even anticipates what we will "get" and not get, and dives into the conversation at exactly the right moments time after time. It is astonishing to watch him do this. A master class in teaching skills. A natural gift and ability to anticipate what we will understand and not understand ahead of time, and to have alternate explanations ready in his quiver. I have never really seen anyone so proficient in this "translation" of material. This is why he is so admired.

They take questions from the audience after it is over, and they answer them with humor, intelligence, and skill. I walk up to Dr. Tyson and introduce myself as the professor who interviewed him by phone recently. He vigorously shakes my hand and implores me to keep him informed on the book's progress. Everyone is standing up now and clapping for them, because they have allowed us an intimate view of the behind the scenes world of physics and scientists and things only a few people in the world know. And now we all know it, and are grateful and proud that they have let us in on it. We also feel like better people; almost more important and empowered than before we came, because they dispelled the myth that science is only for the elite few. It belongs to everyone and we can understand it.

As the crowd leaves, Tyson, with a smile that speaks louder than words, comes up behind and between Jim Gates and Lawrence Krauss, hugs them in with an arm around each of their shoulders, and says to them softly, but loud enough for a few of us to hear; "I love you guys!" And it dawns on me at that moment with a flash of insight so bright that I am surprised when it doesn't light up the dim planetarium; what I have been trying to say throughout this whole book while writing chapter after chapter of what it is that makes a teacher have that "X" factor. When you boil it down, it is simply love. Love for people instead of rules, love for the subject you have devoted yourself to, love for knowledge and of learning. Love—pure and simple.

APPENDIX

EXAMPLE LESSON CONCERNING EINSTEIN'S THEORY OF RELATIVITY (POWERPOINT PRESENTATION)

What Is Gravity?

- According to Newton: the force of attraction between all masses in the universe.
- This "law" has been revised!
- Einstein said that gravity is due to a curvature of "space-time" caused by the matter in it. Planets ride the crest of the curve, causing an orbit. So, what is space-time? It is the "fabric" out of which the universe is fashioned, it constitutes the arena within which the events of the universe take place. Space is not empty! It consists of something!

Definition of Space-Time

So, it is the four-dimensional continuum of one temporal and three spatial coordinates in which any event or physical object is located. North/South, East/West, Up/Down, and Time. Objects travel through time in

The "X" Factor: Personality Traits of Exceptional Science Teachers
pp. 95–100
Copyright © 2010 by Information Age Publishing
All rights of reproduction in any form reserved.

addition to direction. An object standing "still" is still traveling through time.

- Space is not empty as we think it is. It has substance and can be bent by objects that are in it. Think of a bowling ball on a trampoline. The shape of space *responds* to objects in the environment.
- The sun, like a bowling ball, warps the fabric of space surrounding it, the earth's motion is determined by the shape of the warp.
- This effect of the motion of the earth is what we would normally refer to as gravity, but it is really the warping of space. Space grips mass and tells it how to move. This is an orbit.
- Gravity is ALSO caused by the acceleration of the earth through space. We feel heavy in an elevator because we are traveling through space at a high speed.

Source: PBS Online (n.d.-a).

The above grapic demonstrates how the earth and all matter bends the space around it, accounting for the planets' orbits.

- So, all of space is lumpy, bent and warped. Light follows this crooked path. This bending of space is what creates gravity. The more the bend, the more the gravity.
- In 1919, scientists proved this by measuring the bending of light during a solar eclipse in Africa. The light around the moon was bent, proving that objects in space bend the space around them.
- But what if space bent in on itself so much that a "hole" in space was formed? Below is a black hole "swallowing" a star.

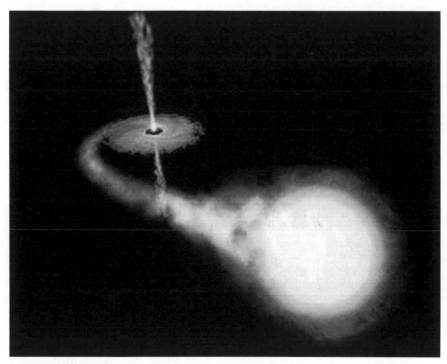

Source: Findpk (n.d.).

Black Holes

- When a star dies, it collapses under the weight of its own gravity to such an extent that all its matter becomes concentrated into an extremely dense object a fraction of its original size. The gravity here is so great, that not even light can escape. Remember—gravity is due to the bending of space.
- Singularity—all matter that falls into a black hole is crushed to a point of zero volume and infinite density. This creates a HUGE amount of gravity!

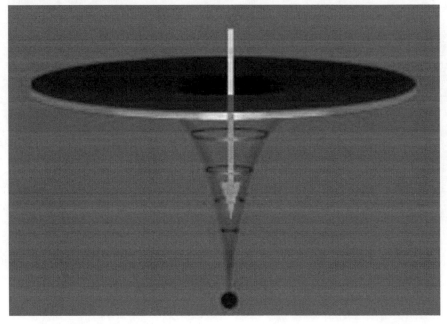

Source: PBS Online (n.d.-b)

- When a star dies, it collapses under the weight of its own gravity to such an extent that all its matter becomes concentrated into an extremely dense object a fraction of its original size. The gravity here is so great, that not even light can escape. Remember—gravity is due to the bending of space.

The Speed of Light: 186,000 Miles Per Second

- Remember when we learned that objects travel through time in addition to direction? An object standing "still" is still traveling through time.
- Einstein discovered that time slows down as we speed up. If we could travel near the speed of light, time would almost stop. Clocks on airplanes run slower than clocks on earth. Why is this? It goes against common sense.

Slowing Down Time

- If you are sitting in a parked car, you are not traveling north/south, east/west, or up/down. But you ARE traveling through TIME. If you begin to travel in your car up the street, you are *diverting* some energy away from TIME and applying it now to n/s, e/w, or up/down.
- So, our watches will run slower than someone sitting still. We can't detect the difference at such slow speeds.
- If we could travel in a spaceship near the speed of light, time would almost stop. This is demonstrated through Einstein's Twin Paradox: two 20 year old twins decide that one of them will travel through space near the speed of light for 50 earth years. The other stays on earth. After 50 years, the space twin returns but hasn't aged at all, the earth twin is 70 years old.

Connecting Science With Literature

Source: http://ircamera.as.arizona.edu/NatSci102/images/alice-rabbithole.jpg and
Down the rabbit hole, Disney: Alice in Wonderland.

Source: Making a Life (n.d.).

REFERENCES

Abdallah, A. (1996). Fostering creativity in student teachers. *Community Review, 14,* 52-58.

Akerson, V. L., & Donnelly, L. A. (2008). Relationship among learner characteristics and preservice elementary teachers' views of the nature of science. *Journal of Elementary Science Education, 20*(1), 45-58.

American Association for the Advancement of Science. (1990). *Science for All Americans; Project 2061.* New York, NY: Oxford University Press.

Artists' Market. (n.d.) Retrieved from http://www.artistsmarket.com/files/u3/escher_smaller_260x260.jpg

Bandura, A. (1977). Self-efficacy: Toward a unifying theory of behavioral change. *Psychological Review, 84,* 191-215.

Banks, J., Cochran-Smith, M., Moll, L., Richert, A., Seichner, K., LePage, et al. (2005). Teaching diverse learners. In L. Darling-Hammon & J. Bransford (Eds.), *Preparing teachers for a changing world: What teachers should learn and be able to do* (pp. 232-274). San Franciso, CA: Jossey-Bass.

Begley, S. (2008, October). Math is hard, Barbie said. *Newsweek, 57.*

Berube, C. T. (2000). A conceptual model for middle school science instruction. *The Clearing House, 73*(6), 312-315.

Berube, C. T. (2004). Are standards preventing good teaching? *The Clearing House, 77*(6), 264.

Berube, C. T. (2008). Atoms, strings, apples and gravity; what the average American science teacher does not teach. *The Clearing House, 81*(5), 223-226.

Berube, C. T. (2009, June 12). Learning about God from fossils. *The Chronicle of Higher Education,* p. A32.

Berube, M. (2002). *Beyond modernism and postmodernism: Essays on the politics of culture.* Westport, CT: Bergin & Garvey.

Bleicher, R. E. (2004). Revisiting the STEBI-B: Measuring self-efficacy in preservice elementary teachers. *School Science and Mathematics.* Retrieved from http://www.accessmylibrary.com/coms2/summary_0286-18309425_ITM

Bloom, B. S. (Ed.). (1956). *Taxonomy of education objectives, the classification of educational goals, handbook 1: Cognitive domain.* New York, NY: David Mckay.

Brown, N. (2004). What makes a good educator? The relevance of meta programmes. *Assessment & Evaluation in Higher Education, 29*(5), 515-533.

Camus, A. (1995). *The first man.* New York, NY: Random House.

Cattell, R. B. (1931). The assessment of teaching ability. *The British Journal of Educational Psychology, 1*(1), 40.

Daugherty, M., Logan, J., & Turner, M. (2003). Associations among preservice teachers' psychological traits and classroom performance ratings. *The Teacher Educator, 38*(3), 151-168.

Doidge, N. (2007). *The brain that changes itself.* New York, NY: Penguin Books.

The Domain for Truth. (n.d.). *What is wrong with this argument?* Retrieved from http://veritasdomain.wordpress.com/2007/06/01/what-is-wrong-with-this-argument/

Dubois, W. E. B. (1968). *The autobiography of W.E.B. Dubois.* New York, NY: International.

Driver, R., Newton, P., & Osborne, J. (2000). Establishing the norms of scientific argumentation in classrooms. *Science Education, 84*(3), 287-312.

Ducharme, E. R., & Kluender, M. M. (1986). Good teachers in good schools: Some reflections. *Educational Leadership, 44,* 43-46.

Ediger, M. (2002). Assessing teacher attitudes in assessing science. *Journal of Instructional Psychology, 29*(1), 25-28.

Eisner, E. W. (1983). The art and craft of teaching. *Educational Leadership, 41,* 4-13.

Findpk. (n.d.). Retrieved from http://www.findpk.com/zahid/UNIVERSE_FILES/Blackhole%20swallowing%20a%20star.JPG

Friedman, H. S., Prince, L. M. Riggio, R. E. & DiMatteo, M. R. (1980) Understanding and assessing nonverbal expressiveness: the affective communication test. *Journal of Personality and Social Psychology, 39*(2), 333-351.

Garza, R. (2009). Latino and White high school students' perceptions of caring behaviors: Are we culturally responsive to our students? *Urban Education, 4*(3), 297-321.

Gilligan, C. (1993). *In a different voice: Psychological theory and women's development.* Cambridge, MA: Harvard University Press.

Gladwell, M. (2000). *The tipping point; how little things can make a big difference.* New York: Little, Brown & Co.

Gladwell, M. (2005). *Blink: The power of thinking without thinking.* New York, NY: Little, Brown & Co.

Gladwell, M. (2008a). *Outliers: The story of success.* New York, NY: Little, Brown & Co.

Gladwell, M. (2008b, December 15). Most likely to succeed: How do we hire when we can't tell who's right for the job? Message posted to: http://www.gladwell.com/ 2008/2008_12_15_a_teacher.html

Glanz, J. (2002). *Finding your leadership style; a guide for educators.* Alexandria, VA: Association for Supervision and Curriculum Development.

Glod, M. (2007, December 5). U.S. teens trail peers around world on math-science test. *The Washington Post.* Retrieved from http://www.washingtonpost.com/wpdyn/content/article/2007/12/04/AR2007120400730.html

Greene, B. (1999). *The elegant universe: Superstrings, hidden dimensions, and the quest for the ultimate theory.* New York, NY: W. W. Norton.

Greene, B. (2004). *The fabric of the cosmos: Space, time and the texture of reality.* New York, NY: Knopf.

Hare, W. (1993). *What makes a good teacher: Reflection on some characteristics central to the educational enterprise.* London: Althouse Press.

Harlen, W. (2006). *Understanding and teaching science.* Retrieved from http://www.scre.ac.uk/rie/nl57/NL57ArticleHarlen.html

Hawking, S. 1988. *A brief history of time.* New York, NY: Bantam Books.

Hofstadter, R. (1963). *Anti-intellectualism in American life.* New York, NY: Knopg.

Hughes, T. M. (1987, November). *The prediction of teacher burnout through personality type, critical thinking and self-concept.* Paper presented at the annual meeting of the mid-South Educational Research Association, Mobile, AL.

Isaacson, W. (2007). *Einstein: His life and universe.* New York, NY: Simon & Schuster.

Jeter, A. (2009, December 12). School board urges closer look: Test irregularities. *The Virginian-Pilot.* Retrieved from http://hamptonroads.com/2009/12/school-board-urges-closer-look-test-irregularities

Jung, C. (1923) *Psychological types.* New York, NY: Harcourt Brace.

Keirsey, D., & Bates, M. (1984). *Please understand me* (4th ed.) Del Mar, CA: Prometheus Nemesis.

Majors, S. (2009, May 31). U.S. students fare poorly in biosciences. *The Virginian-Pilot,* Section Sunday News 2, p. 6.

Making a Life. (n.d.). Retrieved from http://www.makingalife.com/book_covers/johnathanlivingstonseagull.jpg

Meador, K. S. (2003) Thinking creatively about science: Suggestions for primary teachers. *Gifted Child Today, 26*(1), 25-29.

Merriam-Webster Online. (n.d.). *Charm.* Retrieved from http://www.merriam-webster.com/dictionary/charm

MIQEL.com. (n.d.). *Naturally occurring fractals.* Retrieved from http://www.miqel.com/fractals_math_patterns/visual-math-natural-fractals.html

Murphy, C., Neil, P., & Beggs, J. (2007). Primary science teacher confidence revisited: Ten years on. *Educational Research, 49*(4), 415-430.

National Teacher of the Year. (n.d.). Retrieved October 6, 2009 from http://www.ccsso.org/projects/national_teacher_of_the_Year

National Council for Accreditation of Teacher Education. (n.d.). Retrieved from http://www.ncate.org/public/glossary.asp?ch=4#P

Null, G. (1996). *Who are you really? Understanding your life's energy.* New York, NY: Carroll & Graf.

New York Times. (2009, July 19). Share your memories of Frank McCourt. Retrieved from http://artsbeat.blogs.nytimes.com/2009/07/19/share-your-memories-of-frank-mccourt/

Original Beauty. (n.d.). Retrieved from http://originalbeauty.wordpress.com/

Osborne, J. (2009/2010). An argument for arguments in science class. *Phi Delta Kappan, 91*(4), 62-66.

Osborne, J., & Simon, S. (1996). Primary science: Past and future directions. *Studies in Science Education, 27*(99), 147.

Pauley, J. A., Bradley, D. F., & Pauley, J. F. (2002). *Here's how to reach me: Matching instruction to personality types in your classroom.* Baltimore, MD: Paul H. Brookes.

PBS Online. (n.d.-a) *Stephen Hawkings's universe*. Retrieved from http://www.pbs.org/wnet/hawking/strange/html/gravity.htm

PBS Online. (n.d.-b). *Stephen Hawking's universe*. Retrieved from http://www.pbs.org/wnet/hawking/strange/html/blackh.html

Penrose, R. (2004). *The road to reality: A complete guide to the laws of the universe.* New York, NY: Random House.

Princeton University Blog Service. (n.d.). Retrieved from http://blogs.princeton.edu/wri152-3/f05/cargyros/images/picasso_demoiselles.jpg

Ramey-Gassert, L., & Shroyer, M. G. (1992). Enhancing science teaching self-efficacy in preservice elementary teachers. *Journal of Elementary School Science Education. 4,* 26-24.

Schaler, J., & Gardner, H. (2007). *Howard Gardner under fire: The rebel psychologist faces his critics (a blessing of influences).* Chicago, IL: Open Court.

Schussler, D. L., Bercaw, L. A., & Stooksberry, L. M. (2008). The fabric of teacher candidate dispositions: What case studies reveal about teacher thinking. *Action in Teacher Education, 29*(4), 39-52.

Shlain, L. (1991). *Art & physics: Space, time & light.* New York, NY: Morrow.

Smith, R. L., & Emigh, L. (2005). A model for defining the construct of caring in teacher education. In R. L. Smith, D. Skarbek, & J. Hurst (Ed.), *The passion of teaching: Dispositions in the school.* Lanham, MD: Scarecrow Education.

Smith, R. L., Skarbek, D., & Hurst, J. (2005). *The passion of teaching: Dispositions in the schools.* Lanham, MD: Rowman & Littlefield.

Sternberg, R. (2003). *Wisdom, creativity and intelligence: Synthesized.* Cambridge, England: Cambridge University Press.

Sternberg, R. (2009). Teaching for wisdom, intelligence, and creativity. *School Administrator. 66*(2), 10-14.

Temel Nosce. (n.d.). *Heaven and hell.* Retrieved from http://me-damitr.blogspot.com/search?q=Heaven+and+Hell

Think Quest. (n.d.). Retrieved from library.thinkquest.org/.../wr-lightening_jpg.htm

Thornton, B., Peltier, G., & Hill. G. (2005). Do future teachers choose wisely: A study of pre-service teachers personality preference profiles. *College Student Journal. 39*(3), 480 – 496.

Tosun, T. (2000). The impact of prior science course experience and achievement on the Earth science teaching self-efficacy of preservice elementary teachers. *Journal of Elementary Science Education, 12*(2), 21-31. Retrieved from http://www.accessmylibrary.com/coms2/summary_0286-28584726_ITM

WebEcoist. (n.d.). *17 captivating fractals found in nature.* Retrieved from http://webecoist.com/2008/09/07/17-amazing-examples-of-fractals-in-nature/

Wikipedia. (n.d.-a). *Myers-Briggs Type Indicator.* Retrieved from http://en.wikipedia.org/wiki/Myers-Briggs_Type_Indicator#Four_dichotomies

Wikipedia. (n.d.-b). *Frank McCourt.* Retrieved from http://en.wikipedia.org/wiki/Frank_McCourt

Wikipedia. (n.d.-c). *Fractals.* Retrieved from http://en.wikipedia.org/wiki/Fractal

Wikipedia. (n.d.-d). *Mandelbrot set.* Retrieved from http://en.wikipedia.org/wiki/Mandelbrot_set

INDEX